RED LETTER
CHALLENGE

READY TO
CHALLENGE YOUR CHURCH?

WWW.REDLETTERCHALLENGE.COM/CHURCH

TABLE OF
CONT

ENTS

THE WHY BEHIND

THE RED LETTER CHALLENGE

Why does the world around us and the life we live not look anything like the reality Jesus talked about? Why is there no significant difference between the lives of those who call themselves Christians and the rest of the world? What kind of witness can we be in this world if we simply look the same as everyone else? If we are a poor representation of who God is, then what needs to change? What can we do? Rather than shrugging it off, isn't it time to change people's perceptions about the followers of Jesus Christ?

These questions kept bothering me. I kept thinking there has to be something we can do about this. That's when something so simple came to me – something so simple it was genius. What if we take the words of Jesus and actually put them into practice? If we could actually do this, surely that would change people's perceptions about those who follow Jesus!

I know what you are thinking: "That's the big idea?" Yes, that's it. And it wasn't even my idea! That's why I knew it was genius, because I actually stole this idea from Jesus Himself.

Jesus finishes the Sermon on the Mount, the greatest sermon ever preached, by saying this in Matthew 7:24-27:

> *"Therefore everyone who hears these words of mine and puts them into practice is like a wise man who built his house on the rock. The rain came down, the streams rose, and the winds blew and beat against that house; yet it did not fall, because it had its foundation on the rock. But everyone who hears these words of mine and does not put them into practice is like a foolish man who built his house on sand. The rain came down, the streams rose, and the winds blew and beat against that house, and it fell with a great crash."*

Jesus is saying, "If you want your house to stand up, practice what I'm preaching. Do what I say." Jesus says in Luke 11:28: "Blessed rather are those who hear the word of God and obey it." James, the brother of Jesus, says it even more simply in James 1:22: "Do not merely listen to the word, and so deceive yourselves. Do what it says."

That's the big idea. Taking Jesus' words, the ones that are written in red letters in your Bibles, and putting them into practice. Literally. That's the very unoriginal yet revolutionary idea that's going to change not just the followers of Jesus, but the world in which we live!

I looked and looked for something that gave followers of Jesus clear, practical action steps to take what He said and then put those words into practice. There are many great books and resources out there, but I couldn't find anything that organizes the literal words that Jesus spoke and then issues a clear challenge based on that teaching.

I decided this idea needed to be tested. At the time, I was a young pastor in the first full year of a small new church plant. We were looking for ways to get involved in the community and advance the Kingdom of God in our area. Personally, I was trying to awaken the members of my church. You see, at the time, my church was made up mostly of long-time Christians. These were people who had believed in God most of their lives. They were used to church and had gotten into patterns of being surrounded only by Christian friends and serving three or four days a week (but always at the church building). The biggest way they stepped out of their comfort zones was ushering during a church service. Really? People who were forty, fifty, even sixty years into their faith and the way they were being "stretched" by God was by showing someone to a seat, passing an offering plate, and counting heads! My five-year old could have done that - well, as long as the counting didn't go into the hundreds!

However, they were open to trying something new and they were excited about all of the possibilities that might come from it. They were especially eager to see how this Challenge would work. They were committed to doing whatever it took to reach our community, and especially those who didn't believe in Jesus Christ as their Savior.

That's when we implemented the Red Letter Challenge at our church. What would it look like for a whole church, new to the area but excited about the future, to literally practice the words of God together? The results were amazing and lives were changed! The community was changed! The individuals who took part were challenged to new heights in their relationship with Christ, and ultimately our church grew as well. God did incredible things through the Challenge!

People were doing things they never thought were possible. And because we were doing it together, they knew they had the support and accountability of everyone else in the church. We had so many amazing things happen during that first Challenge that we decided to do it again the following year!

I've been blessed by this Challenge. Those who have been through it have been blessed by it. Our church has been blessed by it. Most importantly, our communities were blessed by it and we are changing the perception in our area of who Jesus Christ is. We know this workbook you have in your hands right now is going to bless you and many others if you take this Challenge seriously.

People who are new to the faith have often asked me, "How do I follow Jesus? What am I supposed to do?" Even people who have believed and followed Jesus for much of their life struggle to answer that question. As I explored Christ's words, I found that He asked His followers to do many things, but He spent a good portion of His time focused on five main principles.

1 Being **2** Forgiving **3** Serving **4** Giving **5** Going

We re-organized the Challenge to introduce each of these five principles over the first five days. The following five weeks then focus on each of these principles for one full week. And what you have in your hands right now is the complete 40-Day Red Letter Challenge!

By putting God's words into practice, you will find the life God has made for you! You will be led to spend more time with the God who loves you. You will serve and sacrifice more than you ever have before. You will forgive people you never thought you would be able to. (That person may even be yourself!) You will become a more generous person. You will be more bold and courageous in what you say and in how you live. And through the entire Challenge, you will celebrate and enjoy the life God has given you!

Another thing that will probably happen is you will fail! Sorry for the harsh words. But I've never done the Challenge perfectly. There's been a day I missed here and there or an idea that was too hard for me for a particular day. If this happens to you, I invite you to write down your thoughts for that day and why you struggled. You will find that perhaps you are stronger in some areas than others in your faith.

Being a follower of Jesus is not always pretty, and sometimes we mess up. We have forgiveness for those times and God urges us to come back to Him and keep following after Him. Whether you are experiencing success or failure, I want to encourage you not to get frustrated. Just keep moving on. What we are hoping to create is a new habit in your life. We don't want you to just do what God says for 40 days and then never think about it again. I hope the practice of implementing Jesus' words in your life will become a daily occurrence for you. Habit formation isn't an overnight process. It takes a while. But you have to start somewhere, so let's start with His words and embark together on the Red Letter Challenge!

BY PUTTING GOD'S WORDS LITERALLY INTO PRACTICE, YOU WILL FIND THE LIFE GOD HAS MADE FOR YOU!

HOW TO DO

THE RED LETTER CHALLENGE

Okay, you are ready for the Challenge, but how does it work? What's this going to look like?

The first five days will serve as an introduction. You'll learn a bit more about each of the five major principles from Jesus. From there, on each of the following 35 days, you will see a quote directly from the mouth of Jesus. The quotation will be followed by a devotion, one or more companion Bible readings, and a Challenge of how you might live out those specific words on that day. Some will be very specific and others will be very broad. Each day you will be encouraged to complete the Challenge.

The rhythm of a follower, or a disciple, of Jesus is to be both a hearer and a doer of what God says. That's why for each day there's a corresponding Bible story or passage as well as a Challenge for how to implement Christ's words into your life. Too many followers of Jesus read the Bible but never put those words into practice. Likewise, there are many who do good works but aren't sure why they are doing them.

Putting God's words into practice is much more effective when you are not alone. Many times it is hard to do what God asks. Some of the days you might feel like you want to give up. That's why I suggest bringing someone along with you in this Challenge. Pick someone you trust. Do the Challenge with this person and use each other as accountability partners. Or even better, grab a few friends, your staff, or even your entire church, and invite them to come alongside you on this journey.

We live in an interactive world, and we want to know how this Challenge is going for you and how it is impacting you and your community. This Challenge will move you in many ways. You will have a lot of feelings and emotions as you go through it. This workbook is designed to capture those feelings, thoughts, and emotions. Be honest and fair with yourself as you complete the Challenges.

Finally, I encourage you to post your thoughts on our Facebook page (fb. me/redletterchallenge) and use the hashtag #RedLetterChallenge whenever you are referencing it on any social media platform like Instagram. Let us know how putting God's words into practice went for the day. Was it easy? Was it hard? Why? Why not? Were you unable to complete the Challenge for today? If so, what got in the way?

DOING

THE RED LETTER CHALLENGE AS A CHURCH

Pastors and church leaders, do any of the following apply to you?

1. You want your people to spend more time with God on a daily basis.
2. You want a greater presence in the community in which you serve.
3. You want your people to live greater lives of service and sacrifice.
4. You want your church to be more generous.
5. You want your people to be bolder in their faith.
6. You want your people to experience the freedom that comes from God's forgiveness.
7. You want your church to have active, engaging home groups that meet during the week.
8. You want a resource to point people to after they have received Jesus Christ in their life that gives them very clear direction on what to do next.

I'm betting that many of these apply to you! You are hoping for deeper spiritual formation in your church, yet you know that many people have grown stale in their faith and confuse being disciples of Christ with being volunteers.

This Challenge will awaken the members and attendees at your church.
It will invigorate your church and you will find people in your church doing things they (and you!) never thought were possible!

There is nothing better than a church doing the words of Christ together. **Doing what God asks us to do is not meant to be done alone.**

We have organized small group curriculum as well as full sermon manuscripts and videos on our website (www.redletterchallenge.com), and you can access all of it for free. This Challenge is best done when everyone is not only doing the Challenge on a daily basis by themselves, but also regularly meeting in home groups to discuss the Challenges together. It's also extremely valuable for people to hear you as the pastor talk about the importance of the five main principles as part of a weekend teaching series. Also, we recommend that your church come together at least a couple of times during the Challenge to do what Christ says. Check out the appendix "Community Rally Ideas" for suggestions.

Finally, we want to encourage you as a leader to get fully immersed in the Challenge yourself. If you want your people to invest in it and grow, it's important for you to model it.

WWW.REDLETTERCHALLENGE.COM

WHO IS

THE RED LETTER CHALLENGE FOR?

As the great NBA theologian Allen Iverson once said in a press conference,

"I mean listen, we're sitting here talking about practice, not a game, not a game, not a game, but we're talking about practice."[1]

Okay, so maybe he's not a theologian, but the former NBA star points to a reality that is true for nearly everybody – practice isn't as much fun as the game!

Too many people think that to follow Jesus Christ, they have to wait on the sidelines until they have all of their life in order. They believe they have to wait until they understand the Bible and have read through the entire thing before they can do what He says to do.

I believe **the time to do what Jesus is asking is today**. This Challenge is for you, whether you have been firm in your faith for decades, you've just come to faith in Jesus Christ, or you're wrestling with this whole God thing for the first time.

No matter where you're starting, **doing the words of Jesus will help you**

find the life you were made for. I believe few things stretch our faith more than actually getting involved and doing the things God is asking us to do. When we feel unequipped and unprepared (which you will feel at times in this Challenge), God will use those moments to give, shape, and form your faith.

This Challenge is for anybody and everybody. Young and old. Men and women. Churched and unchurched. New Christian, life-long Christian, non-Christian. It's for anybody who's looking for something more in life.

CHALLENGE EXTENDED!

If I tell my son, "Go clean your room," he's not going to come back a couple hours later and say, "Hey dad, I memorized what you said. You said, 'Go, clean your room.'" And he's not going to say, "Dad, I know 'Go clean your room' in Greek. *Pao Katharos sas domatio*." At this point I'd be impressed, but that's not going to fly! And he's not going to say, "My friends and I are going to gather and study what it would look like if I went and cleaned my room." No, none of that's going to work. So why do we think this is going to work with Jesus?[2]

Jesus said, "Why do you call me 'Lord,' and not do what I tell you to do?" Words without action were never acceptable to Jesus. Faith without action is dead.

On the flip side, there are others (like me!), who enjoy doing. We think just being is boring. We want to get things done! But if we don't spend time being, our doing won't be as productive. If we don't spend the time resting in God and learning from Him, we'll quickly burn out and our activity will become more about us than about Christ.

I remember when I was dating my wife Allison. We went on a trip with her family to the Chicago Science Museum. Allison warned me her dad likes to take 20-minute naps every day, no matter what. Sure enough, he found a bench near one of the displays and curled up and he was out. His eyes were closed, he was snoring, there was drool dripping from his mouth onto the floor. (Okay, I might be exaggerating that last part.)

At this point in my relationship with Allison I was still trying to make a good impression on her family. Apparently they were all used to their dad sleeping in random places, but I was not, so I volunteered to stay with him. People walked by and gave him weird looks, and then they would look at me. I, of course, acted like I didn't know the man. It was very awkward, but right at 20 minutes, he popped up, awake, and I acted like everything was great. I thought it was crazy.

But apparently there is some scientific evidence that says those who take naps during the day can actually be more productive. It doesn't seem like slowing down in the middle of productive work hours would be helpful, but these naps re-energize them so they can get more done.

Psalm 46:10 says, "Be still and know that I am God." Many of us don't know how to just be. We know how to do. But we struggle with the being.

Before we do what Christ asks us to do, we need to be with Him. That's what this first week is all about: Spending time with God. So in our "being" week we will explore what are called spiritual disciplines. These spiritual disciplines are good habits that allow you to more closely connect to Jesus Christ. These disciplines have been practiced for centuries by those who follow Jesus.

The healthiest way to follow Christ and seek Him first is for our doing to flow out of our being. **Our doing flows out of who we are and who we become when we spend time with Christ.**

Here's how I see this playing out in my life:

➡️ When I spend my time with Christ, I can't wait to start doing what He says.

➡️ When I come to church and worship Christ, it gives me the fuel I need to keep going in life.

➡️ When I read the Bible, it doesn't take long for it to manifest itself in me and pretty soon it becomes like a fire shut up in my bones that I cannot contain. I just gotta share it!

➡️ When I pray, there's a peace that comes over me. I can't even explain it.

Jesus said many things when it comes to being with Him. Over the first full week of the Challenge, you'll learn different ways in which you can be with Jesus.

OUR DOING FLOWS OUT OF WHO WE ARE AND WHO WE BECOME WHEN WE SPEND TIME WITH CHRIST.

#REDLETTERCHALLENGE

DAY 2 🤝 FORGIVING

Couches typically look really nice on the outside. But have you ever lifted up the cushions?

Before you do, take a moment to prepare your heart and soul for the horrors you are about to experience. In fact, you may even want to put on a hazmat suit! If you're like our family, you're going to find M&M's, quesadillas, pizza crusts, potato chips, Lego pieces, and possibly the Zika virus. It's all under there.

On the surface the couch looks great. In fact, we've even had people come over and sit on our couch.[3] It looks fine on the surface, but deep down in the cracks is lots of junk.

Our lives are like this. **On the surface many of us look great, but on the inside we are a mess.** We put the highlight pictures of ourselves on social media so everybody thinks everything is great. We look amazing online, so we think we've fooled everybody into thinking we have no major problems in our lives.

We even do this at church. We walk in and act like we're politicians: hugging people, kissing babies, and shaking hands. We try to make everything look flawless, but underneath there's a bunch of stuff we are not so proud of. And sometimes other people can be intimidated because they assume they must be the only ones with a mess under their couch.

The reality is that deep inside each one of us there is a great deal of hurt. All of us carry that around. We're hurting, we're experiencing pain, and many of us are not free because we're held captive to the past. It's like an old couch that we can't get rid of - we keep encountering the mess.

But God doesn't want you stuck in the past, because **if you can't let go of the past you'll never be able to move into the future.** He has taken your mess and nailed it to the cross so you don't have to keep beating yourself up about it. He wants you to experience His grace.

Ephesians 2:8-9 says it perfectly: "For it is by grace that you have been saved, through faith – and this is not from yourselves, it is the gift of God – not by works, so that no one can boast."

In every world religion besides Christianity, you have to do something to have "salvation" or "eternal life." And many of those religions are growing more quickly than Christianity, because they make more sense. Grace is free! We don't deserve grace! So it's difficult to accept.

Brennan Manning says, *"Put bluntly, the American church today accepts grace in theory but denies it in practice. We say we believe that the fundamental structure of reality is grace, not works--but our lives refute our faith. By and large, the gospel of grace is neither proclaimed, understood, nor lived."*[4]

He goes on to say, *"Jesus comes not for the super-spiritual but for the wobbly and the weak-kneed who know they don't have it all together, and who are not too proud to accept the handout of amazing grace. As we glance up, we are astonished to find the eyes of Jesus open with wonder, deep with understanding, and gentle with compassion. This is the God of the gospel of grace."*[5]

My grandpa once talked to a woman in her nineties who had only a couple of weeks to live. She said, "I've been in church my whole life. I've served on every committee. But I don't know if I've done enough good things to enter into heaven. I don't know where I'm going when I die." My grandpa was able to explain to her that she is not saved by what she has done, but by what God has already done. He has already forgiven her of her sins and she can be confident of her salvation.

How sad that a woman can hear all the "right" words and be in all the "right" places for over nine decades and still never truly receive God's forgiveness. I hope that when my grandpa talked to her, she finally felt confidence and assurance in God's grace. Grace assures you that everything has been taken care of. **There is no sin too big that God did not die for on the cross.**

All of us are in desperate need of God's grace. The second full week of our 40-day Challenge will focus on receiving God's forgiveness and learning how to forgive other people.

2/40

THERE IS NO SIN TOO BIG THAT GOD DID NOT DIE FOR ON THE CROSS.

#REDLETTERCHALLENGE

DAY 3 ⚒ SERVING

Yesterday we looked at Ephesians 2:8-9 which says we are saved by God's grace and not by our own works. So if my future has already been taken care of, what is the point of good works? The very next verse says this:

"For we are God's handiwork, created in Christ Jesus to do good works, which God prepared in advance for us to do."

It's no coincidence that the apostle Paul wrote this verse after the previous grace-filled verses. There's a flow to this: once you receive God's grace, you can't help but want to do good. If you are filled with gratitude because someone has helped you, you want to repay that person. It's the same with us and God.

Second Kings 4 is the story of a wealthy Shunammite woman. She made a guest room in her house for the great prophet Elisha. And so one day he says to her, "You have gone to all this trouble. Now what can be done for you?"[6] What I love about this story is she didn't build the room so Elisha would one day do something for her. And Elisha didn't ask her what he could do for her because he had to. They both genuinely wanted to serve the other person.

Far too many people come into a relationship with Jesus just wanting to get more from Him. I get really frustrated when preachers twist the true

Gospel and replace it with a prosperity Gospel that says if you are following Him, God will bless you and you will live a prosperous life. You give this much money and God will take care of your debt, or you do something for someone else and next time you'll get the perfect parking spot.

We don't serve God in order to get more from Him. We've already received Jesus. He is the prize. He is the great reward! We serve God because He first served us.

However, while the motivation behind serving God is not to get more from Him, we always do!

"Just as Elisha actively looked for ways to bless the Shunammite woman, God is eager to bless us. Isn't that a perspective-changing, paradigm-shifting way to look at God? I think most of us imagine that God looks for ways to get us. But what if God is actually dreaming about how He wants to bless you and move on your behalf?"[7]

Our gratitude for what God has done leads us to serve Him. We don't serve God because we have to or because it's how we earn our salvation. We serve God because of everything He's done for us, and for this reason:

While serving others won't save you, it just may help save someone else. Only the Holy Spirit can save someone, but the Holy Spirit lives inside all those who believe in Him. That means He can use someone like you to help save someone else. **You are more powerful than you realize!**

I understand that not everyone in this Challenge is on the same spiritual level. And that's okay. Some of you are doing this Challenge because you feel like you "should." But I hope that over the course of these forty days you realize just how good our God is and how much He's done for you, and your "have to" attitude becomes a "want to."

Jesus had a heart of service. When we serve, we reflect who our God is. A big piece of this 40-day Challenge is changing people's perceptions of Christ-followers. When we serve, when we care for orphans and widows, when we feed the hungry, when we clothe the naked, when we let our lights shine before others, people notice and are drawn to us.

1 Peter 3:15 says, "Always be prepared to give an answer to everyone who asks you to give the reason for the hope that you have." Many times we focus on having the right answers, but before you can give an answer, a question must be asked. We must live our lives so that others will ask, "What is different about that person? Why do they care so much? Why do they serve so much?" And when they ask us, we can tell them we serve because Jesus first served us.

During the third full week of this Challenge, you will begin to serve. You will learn who God calls you to serve and how He calls you to serve.

3/40

WHILE SERVING OTHERS WON'T SAVE YOU, IT MAY HELP SAVE SOMEONE ELSE.

#REDLETTERCHALLENGE

DAY 4  GIVING

Jesus talked a lot about giving. In fact, Jesus talked more about money than He talked about love, heaven, or hell. He talked about money more than any other topic except the Kingdom of God.[8]

Why? Because people desperately need wisdom when it comes to their finances. Many of us are living paycheck to paycheck and drowning under debt. Money is the one thing people argue about most in their marriages. No matter who you are, saving, giving, and managing money is probably a challenge.

So let's start with this statement. You are rich.

Andy Stanley says, *"It's funny, rich people are in denial. And normally we are not in denial about things we know. For instance, tall people admit they're tall. Short people admit they are short. Athletic people admit they're athletic. Artsy people admit they're artsy. And they don't mind telling you that...their car is a mess, their room is a mess, their life is a mess, and they are as happy as can be. Introverts don't even mind telling you they are introverts, and extroverts can't wait to tell you they are extroverts. Like they really need to tell you. But when it comes to rich people, they won't admit it, they live in denial."* [9]

According to statistics, if you make $40,000 a year you are in the top 4% in the world, and if you make over $48,000 a year, you are in the top 1% of earners in the world. We enjoy a quality of life that very few in the history of the world have ever experienced. Our biggest concern is not starvation, but obesity!

However, the more Americans make, the less they give away.

When Allison and I first got married, our apartment was inside a home built around 1900. This apartment only had one very small closet. At this time in history a man probably had one suit and one or two nice shirts. He had some jeans and a couple casual shirts, maybe two pairs of shoes, and that was about it. Ladies, I have no idea what you wore but evidently it would fit in the closet next to those few things. One little closet.

Today it's very different. Our homes have closets in almost every room.

Some have walk-in closets. Some have walk-around closets! And some of us still say we have nothing to wear! Not only that, many of us have so much in our closets that it spills into the garage…and then to clear out our garage we have to store our extra stuff someplace else. I've heard that the storage industry, which barely existed 25 years ago, is now larger than the music industry in our country. There are 52,000 storage facilities worldwide, and 46,000 of those are in the USA. We love our stuff! We are rich. And yet we experience financial problems and stress like never before.

Our priorities have gotten out of whack. When we care more about the stuff we've accumulated than helping out those in need, when we care more about the money we're making than spending time with our family, and when we look to the money in our bank accounts instead of looking to God for our security, we need to totally change our relationship to money.

In the fourth full week of this Challenge, we will see that Jesus challenges His followers to be generous. The more I read the words of Jesus, the more **I'm convinced it's impossible to be a stingy Christian**. We cannot follow Jesus well and at the same time ignore his teaching on money. **If you are truly following Jesus, you are generous.**

And just as we serve out of a response to God, we give because God gave to us. The most famous verse in the Bible is John 3:16: "For God so loved the world that he **gave** his one and only Son, that whoever believes in him shall not perish but have eternal life." God showed His love for us by giving His Son. Jesus showed His love for us by giving up His life. When we give, we reflect the heart and character of our God. The week of giving will definitely challenge you because our "normal" approach to finances is not working. Let's try doing what Jesus asks of us!

I'M CONVINCED IT'S IMPOSSIBLE TO BE A STINGY CHRISTIAN.

#REDLETTERCHALLENGE

When Jesus began His ministry, He moved with an incredible sense of urgency. In the Gospel of Mark, the words "straight away" or "immediately" are used more than forty times. **If Jesus moved with a sense of urgency, then I want to move with a sense of urgency.**

But it's hard to go full-speed for God. We are naturally wired to want to be in control of everything and to go at a comfortable pace. When we decide to follow Jesus, we surrender our need to be in control. It can certainly be scary, but it can also be rewarding, exciting, and adventurous.

Gary Haugen, founder and leader of International Justice Mission, wrote a book called *Just Courage.* In this book, he described something that happened when he was 10 years old that still haunts him today. He describes a day when he was climbing Mount Rainier with his dad and his brothers. He was the littlest, so the climb was difficult for him.

On this particular day, Gary's family wanted to reach Camp Muir, but Gary looked at the huge sign full of warnings for the trail ahead and asked to stay at the visitor's center while they climbed.

His dad agreed, so Gary stayed at the center and explored every corner. But as the day went on, this huge area started to feel rather small. And watching the informational video for the sixth or seventh time wasn't as interesting.

He began to feel rather bored, and sleepy, and stuck.

After the longest afternoon of his life, his dad and brothers finally came back. They were wet from the snow, famished, dehydrated, and nursing scrapes from the rock and ice, but on the long drive home they had stories about an unforgettable day with their dad on a great mountain. Gary says he realized "I went on the trip and missed the adventure."

Gary chose what was easy. It seemed like a fine decision at the time, but in the end it was rather boring. His dad and brothers chose what was hard and had stories, memories, and scrapes they'll always remember![10]

Don't go on the trip and miss the adventure. Many of us want to follow Jesus only whon it's easy and safe The moment it gets hard, we tend to lose faith and question God. But safe and easy makes for a boring story.
In his book *A Million Miles in a Thousand Years*, Donald Miller wrote, *"If you watched a movie about a guy who wanted a Volvo and worked for years to get it, you wouldn't cry at the end when he drove off the lot, testing the windshield wipers. You wouldn't tell your friends you saw a beautiful movie or go home and put a record on to think about the story you'd seen. The truth is, you wouldn't remember that movie a week later, except that you'd feel robbed and want your money back. Nobody cries at the end of a movie about a guy who wants a Volvo.*

But we spend years actually living those stories, and expect our lives to feel meaningful. The truth is, if what we choose to do with our lives won't make a story meaningful, it won't make a life meaningful either."[11]

If you recognized your life was telling a bad story, would you change it? As we start this Challenge, remember you are telling a story. You have the opportunity to tell the story of Jesus by what you do and say during this Challenge. And even though it's not always going to be easy, I guarantee that if you do this Challenge and live by Christ's words, you will be living a story worth telling.

This final week of the Challenge will be tough. God will call you to stretch outside of your comfort zone. On those days, the easy and safe thing would be leaving the Challenge without finishing. But don't go on the trip and miss the adventure!

When God says, "Go," He will always go with you. He will never leave you or forsake you. **When God calls you to go somewhere, you never go alone.** Jesus offers us a way of life filled with adventure, mission, and purpose. Are you ready? Buckle up, the Challenge starts now!

DAYS
6-12

OF THE ☀ 40 DAY

CHALLENGE

WEEK OF

BEING

"COME TO ME, ALL WHO ARE
WEARY AND BURDENED,
AND I WILL GIVE YOU REST."

MATTHEW 11:28

DAY 6

What if I told you God could speak to you at any moment? Sometimes people say, "I just keep waiting to hear God's voice, and I'm getting nothing." **If there was a way to hear from God right now, would you do it?** Of course you would! You would probably do whatever it takes to hear directly from God! Well, the Bible is the book that contains God's words. The Bible is the place where God reveals Himself to you. Yet often the same people who claim to love God so much and who say they want to hear from Him often steer clear of reading the Bible. As a result, they miss out on opportunities to hear from God.

LifeWay Research surveyed more than 2,900 Protestant churchgoers and found that while 90 percent "desire to please and honor Jesus in all I do," only 19 percent personally read the Bible every day.[12] 19 percent. That's pathetic.

Maybe you are a part of the 19 percent who reads the Bible, and if you are, I want to encourage you to keep reading as often as you can. But if the numbers are accurate, that means more than four out of every five people who are going through this Challenge don't regularly read the Bible. How can we truly expect to make an impact for Jesus Christ if we don't even invest some time into reading what He said and growing in our knowledge of who He is?

Listen, I'm not perfect. There are days I fail. My job as a pastor certainly helps keep me in the Bible on a regular basis, but that doesn't mean I'm always learning and growing from God's Word. So this is something even I struggle with at times.

The full quote from Jesus is found in John 8:31-32: "If you abide in my word, you are truly my disciples, and you will know the truth, and the truth will set you free." The word "abide" can mean to dwell or reside. Jesus essentially tells us to live in His Word. He wants us to make the Bible, His words, a part of our life. We are to read, mark, and inwardly digest them. They are to become such a part of us that we can't imagine what our lives were like before we knew the Bible. The Word of God is supposed to go with us wherever we go!

In fact, in the Old Testament, God actually told Ezekiel to eat the Scripture. Ezekiel 3:3 says, "'Feed your belly with this scroll that I give you and fill your stomach with it.' Then I ate it, and it was in my mouth as sweet as honey." God wanted Ezekiel to consume these words so these words would literally take life inside of him. The same is true of us today. God wants us to be reading and studying the Bible so much that the Bible becomes a part of us. His words have the power to actually change us and move us. That's what this Challenge is all about: bringing Jesus' words to life today!

The Bible is the one true story of life. The Bible reveals the one true God: God the Father, God the Son, and God the Holy Spirit. It's in the words of the Holy Bible that we see that through Jesus' life, death, and resurrection we are offered grace, forgiveness, freedom, and new life! Because of this new life, we can't help but want to make a difference and point people to know more about our amazing God. And where do we point them to find out more about God? To the Bible!

There is perhaps no greater spiritual discipline than reading God's Word, because whenever you open its pages, it always accomplishes something. Second Timothy 3:16-17 says, "All Scripture is God-breathed and is useful for teaching, rebuking, correcting and training in righteousness, so that the servant of God may be thoroughly equipped for every good work." Every time you spend time in Scripture, you are being trained, corrected, and equipped. You are always hearing from God!

We'll be doing a lot of good works in this Challenge. The Word of God will prepare us for these good works, because, after all, our doing flows out of our being with Christ.

THE BIBLE
IS THE ONE
TRUE STORY
OF LIFE.

In our Bible reading for today, God calls Ezekiel to be a prophet and speak difficult but true words to the nation of Israel. God is giving the words to Ezekiel to proclaim to the Israelites. Like Ezekiel, we are called to consume God's Word and then share those words and the Gospel message with the rest of the world.

EZEKIEL 2:7–3:4

7 You must speak my words to them, whether they listen or fail to listen, for they are rebellious. 8 But you, son of man, listen to what I say to you. Do not rebel like that rebellious people; open your mouth and eat what I give you."

9 Then I looked, and I saw a hand stretched out to me. In it was a scroll, 10 which he unrolled before me. On both sides of it were written words of lament and mourning and woe.

3:1 And he said to me, "Son of man, eat what is before you, eat this scroll; then go and speak to the people of Israel." 2 So I opened my mouth, and he gave me the scroll to eat.

3 Then he said to me, "Son of man, eat this scroll I am giving you and fill your stomach with it." So I ate it, and it tasted as sweet as honey in my mouth.

4 He then said to me: "Son of man, go now to the people of Israel and speak my words to them.

OPEN THE BIBLE TODAY AND HEAR FROM GOD.

If you haven't ever read the Bible, I would recommend starting in the book of John. John is the 4th book of the New Testament and tells the story of Jesus in a way that helps people understand who He is.

This Challenge today, is a great discipline to practice every day for the rest of the Challenge and thereafter. If you are wondering where to start or how to read the Bible effectively, a great place to start is by downloading the YouVersion Bible App or searching online for a daily Bible reading plan.

Galatians 1-2 ; dying to live in Christ. Following Christ changes you... your old self dies

by focusing on Christian laws we negate the value of Christ saving us by dying on the Cross - it is not the following of rules that redeems us

6/40

DAY 7

Okay, let's just admit it: prayer can be weird! You've seen it. I've seen it. If you want a room of middle school or high school students to be quiet, what do you do? Ask someone to pray. It's amazing how they will quiet down and look at the floor! There's another weird side of prayer as well, and many of you probably know what I'm talking about: The guy who starts praying and enters into another state of intelligence by offering large, verbose, superfluous words you've never even heard come out of his mouth before. Like this one:

"Dear omnipotent, omniscient, and omnipresent God, we beseech thee to justify us through thy vicarious atonement, and sanctify your ekklesia through thy Holy Spirit. Though we inhabit a "simul iustus et peccator" world, we are forever grateful that we receive nourishment and are sustained through the Eucharist. Help us properly exegete the Bible and this world until the coming parousia. Most sovereign, infallible, immutable God, Amen."

Translation: "Hey awesome God, thanks for your grace and continue to guide us with your Holy Spirit until you return! Most awesome God, Amen."

Will Davis, author of *Pray Big*, says, "*Somehow we've gotten the impression that true prayer requires big words, lengthy phrases, and choice theological terms.*"[13] Everything that is said seems to be "just right" and even rhymes. To some degree you are impressed by this, but another part of you is actually turned off. I'm not saying those prayers aren't genuine, but sometimes they can do more harm than good. I think this sort of prayer can actually give a bad impression of what prayer is.

You see, at the heart of it all, **we have a God who desires to have a relationship with us**. Prayer is about being in relationship with God, and God wants you to be who you are. It's not about coming to God with all the right words. It's not about saying everything perfectly. It's about talking, listening, and spending time with Him. And when we spend time with Him, He wants us to be who we are! He doesn't want a fake version of who we think the world wants us to be. He wants you, with all your imperfections, to simply spend time with Him and to grow closer to Him. He wants you to tell Him what's on your mind.

We all come to prayer differently: some of us with good motives, some with bad motives, and some with mixed motives. And that's okay. Prayer isn't pretending that everything is perfect before God. It's not telling God things that aren't true. It's simply being real before Him: telling Him how it is. I'm not saying we shouldn't be respectful, but I'm also saying we shouldn't be afraid to address Him. In fact, in the Lord's Prayer, Jesus teaches us to address God as a father. And so, in many ways, prayer is like me listening and talking with my dad. Richard Foster says, *"Our children come to us with the craziest requests at times! Often we are grieved by the meanness and selfishness in their requests, but we would be all the more grieved if they never came to us even with their meanness and selfishness. We are simply glad that they do come—mixed motives and all."*[14]

Jesus tells us in Matthew 9:38 to pray earnestly. Prayer is such an important part of our journey on this Challenge. Some of the Challenges will be easy; some will be difficult. I'm grateful that no matter how easy or hard the Challenge will be, God is always ready to listen. **Prayer is the most powerful tool we have on this earth**, yet for so many of us it is not a part of our regular daily routine.

It's okay if you don't know exactly how to pray or what to pray. Even Jesus' disciples had to ask Jesus to teach them how to pray. God is glad when you come to Him in prayer. Praying earnestly is the Challenge we are taking up today, but this discipline is truly meant to be a part of our lives every day. Continue to ask God boldly and specifically for the things you desire. The more you come to know Him and spend time in prayer, the more you will find yourself praying for things that you want and that He wants.

PRAYER IS THE MOST POWERFUL TOOL WE HAVE ON THIS EARTH.

We learn from this parable to never give up praying.

LUKE 18:1-8

Then Jesus told his disciples a parable to show them that they should always pray and not give up. 2 He said: "In a certain town there was a judge who neither feared God nor cared what people thought. 3 And there was a widow in that town who kept coming to him with the plea, 'Grant me justice against my adversary.'

4 "For some time he refused. But finally he said to himself, 'Even though I don't fear God or care what people think, 5 yet because this widow keeps bothering me, I will see that she gets justice, so that she won't eventually come and attack me!'"

6 And the Lord said, "Listen to what the unjust judge says. 7 And will not God bring about justice for his chosen ones, who cry out to him day and night? Will he keep putting them off? 8 I tell you, he will see that they get justice, and quickly. However, when the Son of Man comes, will he find faith on the earth?"

SPEND SOME TIME TODAY IN PRAYER. HERE'S A GREAT MODEL:

A Adoration (Tell God what you love about Him)

C Confession (Tell God about the sins in your life and how you plan to turn/repent from them)

T Thanksgiving (Thank Him for His forgiveness and for all the blessings in your life)

S Supplication (Ask Him specific things that you need in your life)

Ask God to give you the strength to make it through this Challenge. Boldly ask Him to strengthen your faith and help you share Him with others.

7/40

DAY 8

Everyone worships someone or something.

I grew up near Memphis, Tennessee. During those years, there was a basketball player known as "Penny" who was lighting up the NCAA with his talent at Memphis State University. In fact, Anfernee "Penny" Hardaway was so good he would later get drafted by the Orlando Magic and team up with Shaquille O'Neal.

I couldn't get enough of "Penny." I went to the basketball camp that he held in Memphis. He once signed a blank sheet of paper for me and I cherished this paper so much. It had a special place in my room that no one was allowed to see or touch. I collected his basketball cards, hung posters of him on my wall, and even bought his basketball shoes which were called the "Air Pennies." (By the way, they are still the coolest pair of basketball shoes ever made.)

I didn't realize it at the time, but I was essentially worshipping Penny. In fact, I thought a lot more about him than I did of the One who created him. Don't get me wrong: "Penny" had a great basketball career that only ended because of injury, and even today, he is known for his charity work. He has a great reputation in Memphis and across basketball. But as great as he was, Anfernee Hardaway is just a man, and one day he will die.

As a child, we can understand this sort of adoration and devotion to a hero or sports star. But there are many of us as adults who still struggle with worshipping the wrong things or people. We worship things that will not last.

➡ Some of us worship a person.

➡ Some of us worship money.

➡ Some of us worship stuff.

➡ Some of us worship sex.

➡ Some of us worship a political party.

➡ Some of us worship our careers.

The definition of worship is: *"The reverent love and devotion accorded to a deity, an idol, or a sacred object."*[15] Many people, even Christians, equate worship with a 60 or 75-minute service on Sunday morning. (Please nothing more than 90 minutes!) And that service certainly is worship. But worship is much more than that. **God is not confined to a building or a time frame, and neither is our worship**. Worship describes who we are 24/7. If to be worshipful means having expressions of reverence and adoration for a deity, doesn't that mean we are, or at least can be, worshipping at all times? Harold Best says, *"We do not go to church to worship, but, already at worship, we join our brothers and sisters in continuing those actions that should have been going on—privately, family, or even corporately – all week long."*[16]

Paul expresses this idea in Romans 12:1. He writes, "Therefore, I urge you, brothers and sisters, in view of God's mercy, to **offer your bodies as a living sacrifice, holy and pleasing to God—this is your true and proper worship."** He's saying that our whole lives are worship. Whenever we reflect the love of God, we are worshipping Him! Martin Luther once said, *"The worship of God…. should be free at table, in private rooms, downstairs, upstairs, at home, abroad, in all places, by all peoples, at all times."*[17]

What they are all saying is that worship happens when I'm around others and when I'm alone. In public and in private. Worship happens when I'm out with friends and when I'm at work. It happens when I'm watching TV, when I'm watching sports, and when I'm online. Worship ought to happen at church with others and at home on my own. No matter where you are or what you are doing you have the potential to be ascribing worth, praise, and glory to God. Everything you do could be an act of worship. Look at your life this way and it will start affecting the everyday decisions that you make! Pretty soon you'll be asking yourself, "If I'm worshipping God right now, would I do this? Would I go here? Would I buy this? What would I do here?" And if you find yourself asking those questions more often, you are on the right track!

GOD IS NOT CONFINED TO A BUILDING OR A TIMEFRAME, AND NEITHER IS OUR WORSHIP.

The Psalms are a great place to see the heart of worship. Psalm 96 is a favorite of mine.

PSALM 96

1 Sing to the Lord a new song;
sing to the Lord, all the earth.
2 Sing to the Lord, praise his name;
proclaim his salvation day after day.
3 Declare his glory among the nations,
his marvelous deeds among all
peoples.
4 For great is the Lord and most
worthy of praise; he is to be feared
above all gods.
5 For all the gods of the nations are
 idols, but the Lord made the heavens.
6 Splendor and majesty are before him;
strength and glory are in his
sanctuary.
7 Ascribe to the Lord, all you families
of nations, ascribe to the Lord glory
and strength.
8 Ascribe to the Lord the glory due his
name; bring an offering and come into
his courts.
9 Worship the Lord in the splendor of

his holiness; tremble before him,
all the earth.
10 Say among the nations, "The Lord
reigns." The world is firmly
established, it cannot be moved; he
will judge the peoples with equity.
11 Let the heavens rejoice, let the
earth be glad; let the sea resound,
and all that is in it.
12 Let the fields be jubilant, and
everything in them; let all the trees of
the forest sing for joy.
13 Let all creation rejoice before the
Lord, for he comes, he comes to
judge the earth. He will judge the
world in righteousness and the
peoples in his faithfulness.

OUR THIRD DISCIPLINE...

IS TO WORSHIP GOD. PEOPLE WORSHIP DIFFERENTLY, BUT MOST PEOPLE THINK OF MUSIC WHEN THEY THINK OF WORSHIP.

Music can help usher us into God's presence and feel things in ways that otherwise we would not. Your Challenge for today is to listen to worship music. Here are a few ways you could do this:

1. Go for a walk and listen to praise/worship music

2. Turn off your phone and computer and read through some Psalms with background music playing

3. Listen to praise/worship music free from distraction

4. Rather than listening to politics, sports, or the top 40, tune into your local Christian radio station on your drives around town

If you need help finding great Christian worship music, I would recommend any of the following: Elevation Worship, Hillsong Worship, Bethel Music, Jesus Culture, and Passion.

8/40

DAY 9

Michael Zigarelli, an associate professor at Charleston Southern's School of Business, polled more than 20,000 Christians of all ages from 139 countries about the busyness of their lives and how it affects their relationship with God.

His report tells us the obvious: we're busy people! In fact, almost 60% of Christians around the world say their hectic lives prevent them from spending time with God. Even more interesting is that pastors are the most likely to say they often or always rush from task to task - beating out business owners, lawyers, teachers, and salespeople!

Writing as a pastor, Zigarelli says, *"But maybe a study like this will wake some of us up to this reality: We, of all people, must find a way to place the Lord above every urgent need, every pressing appointment, every desperate cry."*[18]

You probably don't need statistics to tell you we are busy. It's hard for us to spend significant amounts of time with God.

But when we fill our schedules every minute of the day, we lose focus. We get wrapped up in things that aren't important and just don't matter. My grandfather, who is also a pastor, recently watched a basketball game on TV with me. I am a huge sports fan and so was my grandfather, but over the years, his passion for sports has dwindled. While we were watching the game he said to me, "Sports are interesting, but not important."

I realized I spend a lot of time on interesting but unimportant things. I put a lot of hope, time, energy, money, and passion into following sports, but I am always supporting teams that let me down (I am a Cleveland fan after all!).

Then I realized I also follow a lot of important things in this world, but they too will let me down. Family, friends, job, house, and money are all important, but all of them will let you down at some point.

Some of you have families that ended in divorce, or your kids rebelled against the way you tried to raise them. Perhaps you've been there for your friends when they needed you, but when you needed them, they were nowhere to be found. Some of you have lost jobs. Others bought a house and couldn't keep it. Or maybe you are like me and bought a home only to sell it later and lose tons of money. Speaking of money, it has the potential to let you down, as well. Many of you experienced that in the early 2000's with the economic recession.

My point is that Jesus wants to be our top priority. We fill our lives with interesting and even important things, but fail to create time for Jesus, the most important thing! **We need to say "No" to many good things, so we can say "Yes" to the best thing**. What's amazing is that we spend time, money and energy on things that will let us down, but Jesus will never fail us. He will never leave us or forsake us. We are focused on the wrong things!

Jesus wants us to make Him the most important thing in our lives. In fact, in Luke 14 He demands to be our top priority. We need to get more serious about spending quality time with God, even times of solitude where it's just us and God. In solitude, we purposely abstain from interaction with other human beings and shut ourselves off from other distractions.

Jesus modeled this. Before He made the very difficult decision of which twelve disciples He would choose, the Bible says He went up on a mountainside and prayed through the night. Many times Jesus sought out places to either rest or pray, which were both ways of being alone with God. If Jesus needed this time, how much more do we! Not only do we benefit from spending time alone with God, but He loves it when we come to Him. After all, He created us for His pleasure. It gives Him joy when we make Him a priority. But when we squeeze Him out of our lives and place other things where He should be, it's the opposite of what God wants. This is one area where Christians really struggle. We can do better!

WE NEED TO SAY
"NO" TO MANY
GOOD THINGS,
SO WE CAN SAY
"YES" TO THE
BEST THING.

Here Jesus tells us to hate our families. That's awkward! His point is that if you want to follow Him, you have to put Him first. He asks you to give everything you have for Him, just as He gave everything He had to us.

LUKE 14:25-33

25 Large crowds were traveling with Jesus, and turning to them he said, 26 "If anyone comes to me and does not hate father and mother, wife and children, brothers and sisters—yes, even their own life—such a person cannot be my disciple. 27 And whoever does not carry their cross and follow me cannot be my disciple.

28 "Suppose one of you wants to build a tower. Won't you first sit down and estimate the cost to see if you have enough money to complete it? 29 For if you lay the foundation and are not able to finish it, everyone who sees it will ridicule you, 30 saying, 'This person began to build and wasn't able to finish.'

31 "Or suppose a king is about to go to war against another king. Won't he first sit down and consider whether he is able with ten thousand men to oppose the one coming against him with twenty thousand? 32 If he is not able, he will send a delegation while the other is still a long way off and will ask for terms of peace. 33 In the same way, those of you who do not give up everything you have cannot be my disciple."

SPEND SOME TIME IN SOLITUDE TODAY.

Take your Bible with you and get away from all the distractions.
Try it for 30 minutes and if you are able, do it even longer.

_____

_____

_____

_____

_____

_____

_____

9/40

DAY 10

One pastor said, *"It is now my regular practice to fast before and during the times I preach. I have a deeper sense of dependency on God and of the immense power of the spoken word. This has been demonstrated by the dear individual in my congregation who runs our tape ministry. She said that since January of this year, her orders for sermon tapes have doubled. 'I can't explain it,' she said, 'but whatever it is, keep it up!'"*[19]

I'll have to check with the lady running my "tape ministry" to see if fasting might make any difference for me!

To fast means to abstain from something. Out of all the disciplines we are looking at this week, this one might be the most foreign for us in America.

One time a friend of mine fasted from the mega-tub of popcorn at the movie theatres for the forty days of Lent (the forty days before Easter). This is not really the kind of fast we are talking about here. As much as he tried telling me it was a sacrifice, it wasn't! Also, guys, while it's tempting to fast from doing laundry and chores, that's not what we're talking about here, either!

To truly fast you ought to abstain from something important in your life, something you think you can't go without, something that you will miss. It's in those moments of craving or missing that you can go to God with your thoughts and also thank Him that He does provide for your needs. The hunger or the sense of want for what you're fasting from also reminds you to make Jesus your primary want.

Jesus also tells us that when we fast, we don't do it to get recognized by others. You don't fast to make others say, "Wow, that person is so spiritual," or, "Did you see Bob is giving up food for a week? He must have such a good relationship with God." That's not why we do it. **Fasting** is something you do for your own relationship with God. It is an exercise, a discipline, which **brings you closer to God and helps you realize just how much God provides for you**. That's why He tells us to wash our faces when we fast. The Pharisees would fast and make their faces look disfigured and gloomy so when someone noticed something was wrong, they would be able to talk about how they were fasting. They fasted in order to receive the attention, praise, and glory from man. That's not what Jesus wants when He calls us to fast. He wants us to give up something important and remember that He provides.

It's so easy to get caught up in this world with all of its distractions. There are so many days when I get to the evening and realize, "Wow, I didn't spend any time with God today!" I'm sure I'm not the only one. And when I look back at my day, it all seemed important at the time, but if I'm honest I know that no matter how busy I thought I was, there were moments in the day that I wasted or moments I could have included God.

Fasting is a great way to remember God throughout the day. If you fast from food, for example, you will get hungry, and you will remember why you are not eating that particular day. In that moment, you can go to the Lord and thank Him that He provides for you.

Ultimately God wants our hearts. When we fast, we are giving Him our hearts. We are telling Him, "You are what's most important in my life…all of this other stuff pales in comparison to you. I find everything I need in this world in you."

Many people fast before making difficult decisions. This is a very godly practice. If you've been unsure of a decision, fasting is a good way to clear your mind from worldly things and perhaps receive clarity from God with what He is calling you to do.

Some might choose to fast from food. For others, it might be a fast from television, video games, your cell phone, or Facebook. Some of you may decide to fast for more than a day. Whatever you do, use the time you free up for prayer, and be open to what God might want to do in your life.

FASTING BRINGS YOU CLOSER TO GOD AND HELPS YOU REALIZE JUST HOW MUCH GOD PROVIDES FOR YOU.

These verses mention the kind of fasting the Pharisees were doing versus the kind of fasting God is interested in!

MATTHEW 6:16-18

16 "When you fast, do not look somber as the hypocrites do, for they disfigure their faces to show others they are fasting. Truly I tell you, they have received their reward in full. 17 But when you fast, put oil on your head and wash your face, 18 so that it will not be obvious to others that you are fasting, but only to your Father, who is unseen; and your Father, who sees what is done in secret, will reward you."

GO ON A FAST TODAY.

Make sure you abstain from something that's meaningful to you and will make a noticeable difference in your life not having it. Most people will choose to fast from food, but you could also give up social media, your cell phone, video games, television, etc. As you are fasting, and you think about what it is that you are giving up, use those moments to pray to God and thank Him for His provision in your life.

_____

_____

_____

_____

_____

_____

_____

DAY 11

Now this is something that I can get behind: eating and celebrating! I should make this my life verse! I love to eat and I love to celebrate. Who doesn't love a good party with great food? Amongst all of the grace, forgiveness, love, and healing we see in the life of Jesus, it may be hard for you to imagine Jesus saying a phrase like this. But I would argue that eating and celebrating is why Jesus came! However, before we get to that, let's just call a spade a spade and say that among non-Christians, and even among many Christians themselves, the perception of current-day followers of Jesus is we don't have much fun. A lot of people think Christians are boring and not interesting at all.

Why is that? Jesus talked a lot about food and a lot about celebrating. This was a constant theme for Him. Celebration and thanksgiving for all that God has done is a discipline that ought to be a part of our lives each day.

Yet many people believe that in order to follow Jesus, you have to give up a life of celebration. They believe Christianity in general is restraining. In fact, Emma Goldman once said that Christianity is *"the leveler of the human race, the breaker of man's will to dare and to do … an iron net, a straitjacket which does not let him expand or grow."*[20] That's a pretty brutal assessment of Jesus' followers and sounds nothing like our quote today from Jesus.

People from the outside view Christianity as a set of rules that say we must live a certain way, look the same way, and that we "must not smoke, drink, dance, or associate with those who do." Personally, I think it's sad that people view Christians like this and I think it's our fault for not truly living the way God has made us. John 10:10 tells us that Christ came to give us an abundant life. Too many times we make this life look more boring than abundant!

In his book *Ragamuffin Gospel*, Brennan Manning quotes Robert Hotchkins from the University of Chicago, who says, *"Christians ought to be celebrating constantly. We ought to be preoccupied with parties, banquets, feasts, and merriment. We ought to give ourselves over to veritable orgies of joy because we have been liberated from the fear of life and the fear of death.* **We ought to attract people to the church quite literally by the fun there is in being a Christian."**[21]

I know that if you are following Jesus, your life isn't always easy. Sometimes we go through really difficult times. In fact, Jesus assures us that as His followers we are to expect persecution, suffering, and trials of all kinds. I'm not oblivious to that either. We don't need to walk around with fake smiles. But it's also imperative that we change the world's perception of Christ and His followers. If He gave us an abundant life and if we have all received His grace, then our lives should show it.

The reality is that Christ came to free us to live a life of excitement, adventure, and fulfillment. In Christ, we have received all the grace, mercy, and peace that we could ever want or need. Through the Holy Spirit we have confidence, strength, and power to do things others won't. In fact, if we are honest, **God has already answered all the hard questions in this**

life by sending Jesus Christ. No matter what happens, even in the difficult times, we can have a hope, joy, and peace that those who don't know Christ don't have. Why in the world are we demonstrating that a life with Christ isn't joyful, celebratory, and just overall awesome?

Remember that in the end, after Jesus comes back, we will be with Him forever in heaven. Revelation 19:9 tells us we will be invited to the **wedding feast of Jesus Christ!** We're going to eat and celebrate forever in heaven with our God. Why not practice today?

Today, I want you to celebrate what God has done for you. I want you to live your life with joy and peace today, because that's what Christ has won for you! It's time to embrace the life that Christ has made for you!

WE OUGHT TO ATTRACT PEOPLE TO THE CHURCH QUITE LITERALLY BY THE FUN THERE IS IN BEING A CHRISTIAN.

There are many psalms that express that we have joy in the Lord. Psalm 98 is one beautiful example!

PSALM 98

1 Sing to the Lord a new song,
for he has done marvelous things;
his right hand and his holy arm have
worked salvation for him.
2 The Lord has made his salvation known
and revealed his righteousness to the
nations.
3 He has remembered his love and his
faithfulness to Israel; all the ends of
the earth have seen
the salvation of our God.
4 Shout for joy to the Lord, all the earth,
 burst into jubilant song with music;
5 make music to the Lord with the harp,
with the harp and the sound of singing,
6 with trumpets and the blast of the
ram's horn— shout for joy before the
Lord, the King.

7 Let the sea resound, and everything
in it, the world, and all who live in it.
8 Let the rivers clap their hands, let
the mountains sing together for joy;
9 let them sing before the Lord, for
he comes to judge the earth. He
will judge the world in righteousness
and the peoples with equity.

HAVE SOME FUN WITH THIS ONE TODAY.

Start the day by celebrating and thanking God for five things He has done for you. If you want to keep the good times rolling, throw a party. Call together a few friends or neighbors and eat and celebrate with them!

_____

_____

_____

_____

_____

_____

_____

_____

DAY 12

The Sabbath is one of the most misunderstood among Christians today. Some Christians will go into an interview and say, "I can work whenever." Others will say, "No, Sundays are a deal breaker. I can't work that day." Why do some work and others don't? Why does Chick-Fil-A give up more than $40 million a year by closing on Sundays while almost every other business stays open?

Sabbath is from the Hebrew word which means "rest." It was first used in Genesis 2 after God created the world. God created the world in six days and then rested on the seventh day. Why? Was He tired? No, **God rested because what He made was worth enjoying.** We are created like our Creator, so we also create and rest. We work and we play. **After all, if God takes a day to enjoy his Creation, shouldn't we?**

Have you ever mowed your lawn? Even though it may not have been fun while you were doing it, afterward you took your shower, grabbed a drink, and then just looked at the lawn because you were so proud of your work. This is what Sabbath is like — you are resting and enjoying something you created. This is why God made the Sabbath. We were made to work, but also to rest.

God instituted the Sabbath as a gift for the Israelite people in the Old Testament. God says, "'Above all you shall keep my Sabbaths, for this will be a sign between me and you throughout your generations, that you may know that I, the Lord, sanctify you. You shall keep the Sabbath, because it is holy for you."[22] This was a way the people could prove they were in relationship with God. It was a big deal! People who broke the Sabbath or profaned it in any way were actually supposed to be put to death. Talk about harsh! But remember, the Sabbath was always meant as a gift: an opportunity to rest and enjoy life.

However, by the time Jesus came, the Pharisees had changed the Sabbath into something it was never meant to be. In their desire to uphold the law, they had written chapter upon chapter about what it meant to keep the Sabbath. These were some of the rules they came up with:

➡ You could only eat an egg which had been laid on the Sabbath if you killed the chicken for Sabbath-breaking.

➡ It was not permitted to wear false teeth on the Sabbath (that must have been a hit in the synagogue services).

➡ It was fine to spit on a rock on the Sabbath, but you could not spit on the ground, because that made mud, and that was work.[23]

The Pharisees twisted the Sabbath into something it was never meant to be. You can understand why the Pharisees were so upset with Jesus when it appeared He "worked" on the Sabbath. But Jesus knew what the Sabbath was really about. It wasn't about being miserable and doing nothing. It wasn't about sitting in your house like a bump on a log. It's about enjoying what God has created and what you have created through your work.

Today, we also miss the big idea of the Sabbath. We work all the time because we like the things we get from it – money, possessions, or status. We look to our work to give us some of the things God promises to give.

In Romans 14:5-6, Paul writes, "One person considers one day more sacred than another; another considers every day alike. Each of them should be fully convinced in their own mind. Whoever regards one day as special does so to the Lord."

Paul could have said, "This is exactly how you should keep the Sabbath…" But he doesn't. What he says is that regarding this issue you just have to be convinced in your own mind that you're doing the right thing. Paul isn't telling us to abandon the practice, but to have flexibility in how we live it out. If you take Sundays off, great. If it's Saturday, cool. Maybe one week it's a Tuesday morning with a Thursday afternoon and a Friday evening. As long as your motive is to the Lord and you are enjoying and resting in His creation then it doesn't matter when you do it. Just make sure you do it. **The more we keep the Sabbath, the more we will find the life we were made for.**

IF GOD TAKES A DAY TO ENJOY HIS CREATION, SHOULDN'T WE?

Here we read the story of Jesus upsetting the Pharisees on the Sabbath. He had just picked some heads of grain and the Pharisees accused Him of being unlawful.

MARK 2:25–3:6

25 He answered, "Have you never read what David did when he and his companions were hungry and in need? 26 In the days of Abiathar the high priest, he entered the house of God and ate the consecrated bread, which is lawful only for priests to eat. And he also gave some to his companions."

27 Then he said to them, "The Sabbath was made for man, not man for the Sabbath. 28 So the Son of Man is Lord even of the Sabbath."

3:1 Another time Jesus went into the synagogue, and a man with a shriveled hand was there. 2 Some of them were looking for a reason to accuse Jesus, so they watched him closely to see if he would heal him on the Sabbath. 3 Jesus said to the man with the shriveled hand, "Stand up in front of everyone."

4 Then Jesus asked them, "Which is lawful on the Sabbath: to do good or to do evil, to save life or to kill?" But they remained silent.

5 He looked around at them in anger and, deeply distressed at their stubborn hearts, said to the man, "Stretch out your hand." He stretched it out, and his hand was completely restored. 6 Then the Pharisees went out and began to plot with the Herodians how they might kill Jesus.

TAKE A DAY OFF!

Use this day to enjoy what God has given you. It could be your faith, your family, or your house. In addition, what do you enjoy doing? Spend some time doing a hobby or pursuing an interest. Enjoy the day but don't be too legalistic about it, and at some point spend some time reading your Bible and praying. If you can't take today off, intentionally take one of the next seven off. What did you do? How did you rest and enjoy this world?

_____

_____

_____

_____

_____

_____

_____

12/40

13-19
OF THE 40 DAY
CHALLENGE

WEEK OF

FORG

IVING

"BE KIND AND COMPASSIONATE
TO ONE ANOTHER, FORGIVING
EACH OTHER, JUST AS IN CHRIST
GOD FORGAVE YOU."

EPHESIANS 4:32

DAY 13

The very first thing Jesus says to begin His ministry is "Repent and believe the good news." Before Jesus serves, teaches, preaches, or heals He first invites people to receive the grace He has won for all of them. And before we start to forgive others and begin serving, giving, and going, we need to understand the good news of Jesus Christ.

I had a really rough week earlier this year. I was driving home with my kids and all of a sudden I saw the flashing lights from a motorcycle behind me. There are never cops in my neighborhood, so this was quite a shock! I pulled over and the cop asked for my license and registration. It was dark and late, and I was hoping the cop would see my kids and realize that I needed to get home and get them in bed. But no. He gave me a speeding ticket and mentioned he took it down from 12 above the speed limit to 10. I said thanks, but in my heart I was not grateful one bit.

The next morning, I was driving our other car to work and, wouldn't you know it, I got pulled over again in my neighborhood – by the same cop! I rolled down the window and he said, "You again?" And I said, "Good to see you again, officer!" Apparently I didn't fully stop at a stop sign. He asked where I was rushing off to and what I was doing. I told him I was a pastor and he said, "You realize I gave you some grace yesterday, right?" I said, "Yes," but in my heart I was thinking, "Officer, I don't think you understand what grace is. Grace is a free gift given to someone who doesn't deserve it, not a partial gift." He went back to his car and I began praying, "Please God, not another ticket. I really don't want to tell my wife I got two tickets in less than ten hours." Turns out my prayer was answered because I was given two tickets, one for running a stop sign and one for not having an active registration! In a ten-hour period I was given three tickets. I was really bummed.

I reached out to one of my friends who is a lawyer. I told him I was guilty but it was going to cost a lot of money and I also didn't want all those points on my record. He said, "Give me the tickets and I'll take care of them." I asked him what I needed to do. He said, "Nothing, I'll take care of them for you." I didn't ask any questions and didn't quite understand the process. How are you going to wipe away my tickets when I know I was at fault? He encouraged me to stop asking questions and just give him the tickets. Two months later, the day of my court date, he told me it had all been taken care of. Not guilty. No fine. Done. The officer didn't even show up. I was guilty, and yet I was pardoned!

This is a picture of God's grace for us. **We are all guilty – that includes you.** The apostle Paul says in Romans 3:10 that "There is no one righteous, not even one." Sometimes we don't really believe that our sin is that big of a deal, but we have all sinned.

On the other hand, others of us wallow in our mistakes and think we are beyond forgiveness. **Yet no matter how serious, big, or awful your sin is, God's grace extends to cover it.**

God, who is our Judge, says in spite of your faithlessness, He will be faithful. In spite of our addiction, Jesus came to set us free. In spite of the chaos and turmoil of our circumstances He came to bring us peace. And like a judge, He has the power to overrule our objections. When our hearts object and say we could never be forgiven, God says, "Objection overruled," because the blood of His Son Jesus is powerful enough, pure enough, and strong enough to cover all of your sins.

We are guilty, and yet through Christ's grace we are free. That freedom then influences the way we live the rest of our lives!

Before we can forgive others, we first need to spend a couple of days realizing that we personally need Christ's forgiveness as much as anyone else. Thank you, Jesus, for the grace that you offer to us all!

NO MATTER HOW SERIOUS, BIG, OR AWFUL YOUR SIN IS, GOD'S GRACE EXTENDS TO COVER IT.

This story reminds us that no one is outside the reach of Jesus Christ! Saul was an influential politician that approved of the murders of many Jesus-followers. He would be the least likely of candidates to receive God's grace. But on the Damascus Road, as Saul was on the way to persecute more Christians, Jesus caused him to go blind and this conversation ensued:

ACTS 9:4-9, 15-19

4 Paul fell to the ground and heard a voice say to him, "Saul, Saul, why do you persecute me?"

5 "Who are you, Lord?" Saul asked.

"I am Jesus, whom you are persecuting," he replied. 6 "Now get up and go into the city, and you will be told what you must do."

7 The men traveling with Saul stood there speechless; they heard the sound but did not see anyone. 8 Saul got up from the ground, but when he opened his eyes he could see nothing. So they led him by the hand into Damascus. 9 For three days he was blind, and did not eat or drink anything.

God then speaks to one of His prophets named Ananias who lives in Damascus. He tells him to go pray for Saul and to restore His sight. Ananias is confused, because of all that he had heard about Saul.

15 But the Lord said to Ananias, "Go! This man is my chosen instrument to proclaim my name to the Gentiles and their kings and to the people of Israel. 16 I will show him how much he must suffer for my name."

17 Then Ananias went to the house and entered it. Placing his hands on Saul, he said, "Brother Saul, the Lord—Jesus, who appeared to you on the road as you were coming here—has sent me so that you may see again and be filled with the Holy Spirit." 18 Immediately, something like scales fell from Saul's eyes, and he could see again. He got up and was baptized, 19 and after taking some food, he regained his strength.

AS WE START OUR WEEK OF FORGIVENESS...

WE WANT TO FOLLOW JESUS' EXACT WORDS: REPENT AND BELIEVE IN THE GOSPEL.

To repent means that we are truly sorry and ready to turn away from our sin. As we repent and acknowledge that we are sinners, we also receive and believe the good news that Jesus Christ has grace for us!

Repentance is not a one-time prayer. It's an everyday practice. If you are ready to repent and be forgiven, say this prayer:

Dear Lord Jesus, I know that I am a sinner, and I ask for Your forgiveness. I believe You died for my sins and rose from the dead. I turn from my sins and invite You to come into my heart and life. I want to trust and follow You as my Lord and Savior. In Your Name. Amen.

If that was the first time you ever said that prayer, please email us at **hello@redletterchallenge.com** and let us know. We'd love to send you some FREE online resources!

13/40

DAY 14

To display the shocking nature of grace we are going to look at a story in John 8. You'll need to read the Bible story now to better understand the context of our devotion today.

JOHN 7:53–8:11A

53 Then they all went home, 1 but Jesus went to the Mount of Olives.

2 At dawn he appeared again in the temple courts, where all the people gathered around him, and he sat down to teach them. 3 The teachers of the law and the Pharisees brought in a woman caught in adultery. They made her stand before the group 4 and said to Jesus, "Teacher, this woman was caught in the act of adultery. 5 In the Law Moses commanded us to stone such women. Now what do you say?" 6 They were using this question as a trap, in order to have a basis for accusing him.

But Jesus bent down and started to write on the ground with his finger. 7 When they kept on questioning him, he straightened up and said to them, "Let any one of you who is without sin be the first to throw a stone at her." 8 Again he stooped down and wrote on the ground.

9 At this, those who heard began to go away one at a time, the older ones first, until only Jesus was left, with the woman still standing there. 10 Jesus

straightened up and asked her, "Woman, where are they? Has no one condemned you?"

11 "No one, sir," she said.

"Then neither do I condemn you," Jesus declared.

The Pharisees had spent months hatching the perfect plan to trap Jesus. This was the moment they were waiting for. "Jesus," they said, "the Law tells us this woman has to be punished. What do you say?"

This is a tough question. They've caught Him in a contradiction in front of His disciples. If He answers, "Yes, stone her," that seems to go against everything He's been teaching. But if He says, "No, don't stone her," He would seem to be relaxing His morals. It's a tough question, but **God can handle tough questions.** These cunning hypocrites were overmatched.

Before Jesus answers, He bends down and doodles in the dirt with His finger. So they kept on questioning him. And finally Jesus responds to their inquiry, "Let any one of you who is without sin be the first to throw a stone at her."

Silence comes on the crowd. Somehow Jesus sneaked His way out of this situation. He goes back to doodling again on the ground and all the people start leaving.

Scholars have debated what Jesus wrote on the ground. Some think Jesus was writing down a Bible verse. I'm sure He knew quite a few of them, right? Others think He was writing down some of the commandments. Others suggest He started writing down the names of the people who were standing in that circle holding stones, and then listing their sins. It says the older ones left first. Why? Because they had the longest list, right?! In a sense, Jesus is saying, "You want to talk about dirt? Let's talk about dirt. I know some stuff about you."

The reality is there is only one person left who is without sin, and that's Jesus. What's He going to do?

Sometimes people have the impression God is out to get us or He's angry with us. Christians have even been known to advance this way of thinking. In fact, if I were to look at all the Christian billboards and signs I'd think God hated someone like me. I wouldn't want to come to church or approach Him, because He'd punish a person like me. I wouldn't want to come to church or the roof might cave in on me after all that I've done wrong.

But that's not who our God is. In fact, John 3:17 tells us that, "Jesus did not come to condemn the world, but to save the world."

Jesus could have picked up a rock and thrown it at this woman. He would have been justified according to the Law. But in this story, Jesus' eyes are not focused on finding a rock. Instead, His eyes are filled with mercy and love for this woman. Jesus didn't begin by accusing her, and He's not going to start by accusing you.

The devil will try to accuse you. He will throw his rocks at you and remind you of what you have said and done and left undone. **The problem is that many of us spend much more time listening to the accusations of the enemy than to the truth of the Gospel.**

The only one who had a rock to throw didn't even pick one up. Instead, Jesus got down in the dirt for her, and He got down in the dirt for you. He forgave my sins.

He's wiped my past clean. He's clothed me with His righteousness. By His stripes I am healed.

God isn't afraid of your past. He's not afraid of where you've been and who you've hung out with. God loves you for who you are. He'll take you as you are. Some of you think you are too dirty for God. When Jesus Christ died on the cross, **He died for all the sins of every man and woman who has ever lived, is living, and will ever live.**

You have been forgiven! And as forgiven people, we are to emulate Jesus. If Jesus dropped His rock for us, we need to drop our rocks as well. We are here to help save others and not to condemn them.

Drop your rock – for others, and for yourself.

Can you forgive others? What about forgiving yourself? Are you still holding onto things you've done? If you think your sin is too great for Him to forgive, you are actually stripping away the power of the cross. Jesus came to seek and save those who were lost, and that includes all of us.

THIS IS THE DAY TO DROP OUR ROCKS.

Most of us have certain sins that really bother us. Which sins do you elevate above the rest? Write those sins on the rocks on the next page and pray that you are able to see all people, no matter what their sins might be, as candidates for the grace of Jesus Christ.

_____

_____

_____

_____

_____

_____

_____

_____

14/40

DAY 15

JUDGE NOT
MATTHEW 7:1

If you ask me to describe God, I think of grace. The Gospel is the Good News that Jesus Christ came to give us all grace, and that by His grace we are saved.

Grace is a free gift from God. The grace of God comes to us from the cross where Jesus took our sin on Himself. This gift of grace calls us to live a life like Jesus.

If grace is getting something we don't deserve, the opposite would be getting something you do deserve, and that's called judgment. And the church is known for being judgmental. It's one of the first words many people use to describe the church.

If God is known for grace, shouldn't the church be known for grace? Then why are followers of Jesus known for the exact opposite?

That frustrates and saddens me. How in the world could the church be known for being the exact opposite of the God it worships?

It's been said the most frequently quoted Bible verse today isn't John 3:16. It's Matthew 7:1: "Judge not unless you want to be judged."[24]

Non-believers are scared to walk in the doors of our churches or to hang around "Christian" people because they're afraid of what we're going to think about them.

I remember a commercial from several years ago. A man is preparing dinner. He chops vegetables with a large knife while tomato sauce simmers on the stove. A white cat knocks the pan of sauce onto the floor and then falls into the mess. Just as the man picks up his tomato-splattered cat, his wife opens the door. She sees him holding a cat dripping with red sauce in one hand and a large knife in the other.

Things aren't always as they first appear.

A few years ago a grocery store clerk wrote to Ann Landers, a famous advice-columnist. She said she had seen people buy "luxury" food items—like birthday cakes and shrimp—with food stamps. The writer said she thought people on welfare who treated themselves to such non-necessities were "lazy and wasteful."

A few weeks later this appeared in the Ann Landers column:

"I'm the woman who bought the $17 cake and paid for it with food stamps. I thought the woman in the store would burn a hole through me with her eyes. What she didn't know is the cake was for my little girl's birthday. It will be her last. She has bone cancer and will probably be gone within six to eight months."

You never know what other people are dealing with.

Right after that verse in Matthew 7, Jesus says, "Why do you notice the speck of sawdust in your brother's eye, when you've got a plank in your own eye?"[25]

This is one of the most sarcastic sayings of Jesus. And I love it!

If you get a bug in your eye, it's a pretty big nuisance. Your sight gets blurry, and your eyes start to itch.

Now imagine actually having a plank in your eye. If you suffer because of a bug, think about having a plank! Everyone would see it. It would knock into people. You'd lose all sight in that eye! Wouldn't you do everything you could to take it out? Removing it would be the focus of your every thought. And what Jesus is teaching you is that you have an opportunity, through the grace Jesus won for you, to live a life without that plank - and instead you are worried about a little speck of dust in someone else's eye!

Rather than seeing everything wrong with everybody else, God is giving us an opportunity to love people. He has removed your plank by the precious blood of Jesus and He gives you an opportunity to share that Good News with everyone else.

What if, rather than judging people, the church was known for embracing people where they are? What if we stopped trying to change people and just accepted them? What if we remembered it's the Holy Spirit's job to change them, not ours?

It is not your job to judge other people or the dust in their eyes. Your job is to love people the way God loves you!

IF GOD IS KNOWN FOR GRACE, HOW CAN WE, HIS FOLLOWERS, BE KNOWN FOR JUDGMENT, THE EXACT OPPOSITE?

#REDLETTERCHALLENGE

Here is the quote in the context of Jesus' teaching.

MATTHEW 7:1-5

"Do not judge, or you too will be judged. 2 For in the same way you judge others, you will be judged, and with the measure you use, it will be measured to you. 3 "Why do you look at the speck of sawdust in your brother's eye and pay no attention to the plank in your own eye? 4 How can you say to your brother, 'Let me take the speck out of your eye,' when all the time there is a plank in your own eye? 5 You hypocrite, first take the plank out of your own eye, and then you will see clearly to remove the speck from your brother's eye.

NAIL A PLANK IN YOUR EYE
AND WALK AROUND WITH IT TODAY AND CHECK OUT HOW PEOPLE REACT. OKAY, JUST KIDDING!
TODAY, I REALLY WANT YOU TO DO TWO THINGS:

1 Thank God for the opportunity we have to live a plank-free life without the judgment we deserve.

2 Write down the names of any individuals or groups of people you might have improperly judged in the past and ask God for forgiveness.

_____

_____

_____

_____

_____

15/40

DAY 16

Today, Jesus asks us to be merciful just as the Father is merciful towards us. We are not really in a culture where we practice mercy very often. The definition of mercy is, *"Compassion or forgiveness shown toward someone whom it is within one's power to punish or harm."*[26] But, if we are honest, a lot of times we don't like to show compassion or forgiveness. We prefer to get revenge.

We crave fairness and equality. We kind of like the theory of "an eye for an eye" and "a tooth for a tooth." If you look at the TV shows or movies we watch, revenge is all over the place! In fact, not long ago there was a new show on television called "Revenge." The summary of the show says it centers on a young woman who is welcomed into a community filled with people who don't know she's only there to exact revenge on those who had destroyed her family. Her whole life is about revenge. Countless movies are all about revenge, too: The Count of Montecristo, Karate Kid, Gladiator, the Break-Up, Mean Girls, Payback, Kill Bill, Man on Fire, and Taken – just to name a few!

There are two approaches to revenge in our day:

1 Direct Approach: The direct approach is: "You do something bad to me, I'll do something bad to you." If you do something bad to me, I will punch you in the face, I will shoot you, I will impale you, or if it's a really good movie I'll do all of the above!

2 Indirect Approach: The indirect approach is: "You do something bad to me, I'm going to live my life so well that in comparison to me, people will laugh at you." You see this sort of revenge enacted often at high school reunions. Someone made fun of you or bullied you in high school, and now you want to come back at the reunion and show them how much greater you are now.

But we have a God who doesn't work this way. He forgives time and time again, and calls all of His disciples to do the same. He forgives us every time we come to Him. **There is endless mercy for us in Jesus.**

Often I hear the words grace and mercy used synonymously with one another. They are close but they are not identical. **To receive grace is to receive a gift you do not deserve. To receive mercy is to not receive something you do deserve.** I've heard the word grace summarized as, "God's Riches At Christ's Expense." Grace is the eternal life we have with God despite the fact that we have not earned it by our own works. It's a free gift and we don't deserve it. So in essence the gift of grace from God results in heaven for those who believe.

Mercy, on the other hand, is not having to endure the punishment we all deserve. We have all messed up and fallen short of God's glory and deserve death and the consequences of hell. **God had every right to punish us or harm us. He had every right to throw us where we belong, but instead He had mercy on us.** If grace means heaven, mercy means "not hell." Another example of mercy would be if I break the law or am caught speeding and the police officer doesn't hold me to it. He has mercy on me and forgives me of my ticket.

I'm thankful we have a God who is not vengeful, but instead is full of mercy. It's only because of His mercy that we are saved from having to face the ultimate punishment in hell. God now calls us to be like Him, to put whatever someone else deserves to the side, and instead show them mercy. It's through forgiveness and compassion that people come to know Jesus. May you be a person that brings that forgiveness and compassion to others in your life today!

GOD HAD EVERY
RIGHT TO PUNISH
US OR HARM US. HE
HAD EVERY RIGHT TO
THROW US WHERE
WE BELONG, BUT
INSTEAD HE HAD
MERCY ON US.

If we have been forgiven millions, how could we not forgive thousands? We have been given mercy for our sin and Christ calls us to forgive others, as well.

MATTHEW 18:21–35

23 "Therefore, the kingdom of heaven is like a king who wanted to settle accounts with his servants. 24 As he began the settlement, a man who owed him ten thousand bags of gold was brought to him. 25 Since he was not able to pay, the master ordered that he and his wife and his children and all that he had be sold to repay the debt.

26 "At this the servant fell on his knees before him. 'Be patient with me,' he begged, 'and I will pay back everything.' 27 The servant's master took pity on him, canceled the debt and let him go.

28 "But when that servant went out, he found one of his fellow servants who owed him a hundred silver coins. He grabbed him and began to choke him. 'Pay back what you owe me!' he demanded.

29 "His fellow servant fell to his knees and begged him, 'Be patient with me, and I will pay it back.'

30 "But he refused. Instead, he went off and had the man thrown into prison until he could pay the debt. 31 When the other servants saw what had happened, they were outraged and went and told their master everything that had happened.

32 "Then the master called the servant in. 'You wicked servant,' he said, 'I canceled all that debt of yours because you begged me to. 33 Shouldn't you have had mercy on your fellow servant just as I had on you?' 34 In anger his master handed him over to the jailers to be tortured, until he should pay back all he owed.

35 "This is how my heavenly Father will treat each of you unless you forgive your brother or sister from your heart."

BE INTENTIONAL ABOUT SHOWING MERCY TO SOMEONE TODAY.

Perhaps you can let someone off the hook if they owe you a favor or some cash. If you don't have the opportunity today, be on the lookout for someone you can show mercy to at some point this week.

_____

_____

_____

_____

_____

_____

16/40

DAY 17

This quote from Jesus is one of the most difficult Challenges. It's really hard to forgive other people. But it's even worse to continue holding onto things that keep us from being who God has created us to be.

To forgive means to let go of something and give it to God because you believe He will enact better justice than you could. It's the opposite of taking revenge. Jesus mentions forgiveness often - and He lives by it, too. Jesus follows this way of forgiveness all the way to the cross, and even on the cross He forgives the people who are killing Him. "When Jesus prayed for His enemies to be forgiven as they drove nails into His hands, He was living His own sermon, and validating His right to preach it."[27] So if we truly want to follow Jesus, we have to be people who forgive.

There's nothing that can be done to us or against us that we cannot forgive.

At least that's what we say. But what about this situation?

Simon Wiesenthal was an Austrian Jew imprisoned in a Nazi concentration camp. He worked in a hospital where a young German soldier named Karl Seidl was about to die. Seidl's last request was to talk to a Jew. Karl had been mortally wounded and wanted to make a deathbed confession. For several hours he pours out his heart about how sorry he is for all the things he has done. He mentions people he has killed, and Simon knows some of the victims are his family and friends.

After hours of confessing, Seidl asked if Wiesenthal could forgive him. In his book *The Sunflower*, Wiesenthal asks:

"Ought I to have forgiven him? Was my silence at the bedside of the dying Nazi right or wrong? This is a profound moral question that challenges the conscience of the reader of this episode, just as much as it once challenged my heart and mind...The crux of the matter is, of course, the question of forgiveness. Forgetting is something that time alone takes care of, but forgiveness is an act of volition, and only the sufferer is qualified to make the decision. You, who have just read this sad and tragic episode in my life, can mentally change places with me and ask yourself the crucial question, 'What would I have done?'"[28]

The rest of his book includes 53 different prominent thinkers weighing in on whether he should forgive him. 28 of the authors said forgiveness is not possible, 16 said it is, and nine were unsure. How would you respond?

As followers of Jesus we are called to forgive, but even in this situation? Or is this an exception to the rule? Is there a limit to forgiveness? It's a question we can all relate to because we have all been wronged by somebody.

In Matthew 18, Peter asks Jesus how many times we have to forgive a person. Do we have to forgive seven times? Jesus replies, "I tell you, not seven times, but 77 times."

Peter was looking for a limit. He thought he was being generous by suggesting seven times, because the Law only required three. But Jesus' response took it to the extreme. Other translations say 70 times 7. All scholars believe that either way, Jesus wasn't being literal. Instead, these numbers suggest a never-ending limit on forgiveness. Because the numbers 70 and seven signify perfection and completion, they suggest we ought never be done forgiving someone.

My favorite story of forgiveness is when Jesus forgives Peter for denying Him three times. Peter was one of Jesus' best friends and he let Jesus down at the moment Jesus needed him most. Yet Jesus forgives Peter three times for denying Him and then puts him right back to work with the most important job ever: to lead the first church! It's one thing to forgive, but it's another thing to completely trust someone and give them the greatest responsibility in the world!

God showed us the essence of who He is when Jesus died for all of our sins. Now He calls us to be like Him. To forgive somebody is not only good for that person, but it's good for you, too. When you forgive you become more like Christ.

THERE'S NOTHING THAT CAN BE DONE TO US OR AGAINST US THAT WE CANNOT FORGIVE.

In John 18:15-18, Peter denies Jesus three times. Then in John 21, after Jesus rises from the dead, He meets Peter again. Rather than rebuking him, Jesus forgives Peter and charges him with the task of being the leader of the church!

JOHN 21:15-19

15 When they had finished eating, Jesus said to Simon Peter, "Simon son of John, do you love me more than these?"

"Yes, Lord," he said, "you know that I love you."

Jesus said, "Feed my lambs."

16 Again Jesus said, "Simon son of John, do you love me?"

He answered, "Yes, Lord, you know that I love you."

Jesus said, "Take care of my sheep."

17 The third time he said to him, "Simon son of John, do you love me?"

Peter was hurt because Jesus asked him the third time, "Do you love me?" He said, "Lord, you know all things; you know that I love you."

Jesus said, "Feed my sheep. 18 Very truly I tell you, when you were younger you dressed yourself and went where you wanted; but when you are old you will stretch out your hands, and someone else will dress you and lead you where you do not want to go." 19 Jesus said this to indicate the kind of death by which Peter would glorify God. Then he said to him, "Follow me!"

IF YOU'VE STILL BEEN WITHHOLDING FORGIVENESS FROM SOMEONE WHO HAS DONE YOU WRONG.

Pray to God about forgiving that person. After praying, if it can be beneficial, reach out to whoever it might be who has wronged you and let that person know of your forgiveness.

17/40

DAY 18

LOVE YOUR ENEMIES AND PRAY FOR
THOSE WHO PERSECUTE YOU
MATTHEW 5:44

Maybe you've heard this phrase: "Do not hate your enemies; instead, pray for your enemies because it's super passive-aggressive and will totally tick them off." While this is funny, it's not why we pray for or love our enemies. We don't do it to make them feel worse. We do it because we want to live like Jesus. Jesus calls us to a lifestyle that might seem weird to the rest of the world. It's weird to say "I'm going to love my enemies and pray for them." It's even weirder to actually do it! The world says to hate our enemies or seek revenge on them. Jesus is calling us to do the opposite.

During seminary, I was blessed to lead a college ministry at Saint Louis University. We had worship services on Saturday evening and one night I preached a sermon I felt really, really good about. We had a packed house, the energy was high, and I was passionate about my topic. Five different seminary professors were there. It wasn't unusual to have a professor or two in attendance, but this was a few more than normal. I was proud because I knew I had just preached one of my best sermons ever. Or so I thought!

Two weeks later my supervisor called me to his office, and one of the professors who had been at the service was there to talk to me about my sermon. I thought, "Great, he must have really liked it. Maybe he wants me to preach it somewhere else."

Nope! He hated it. While we talked, he criticized my theology, claimed there was no Gospel in it, and called my "performance" narcissistic. He didn't think I was fit to be a pastor and required me to take an additional Law and Gospel class at the seminary.

After our conversation, I figured everything would just go away. But it didn't. This professor wanted to make an example out of me. My other professors told me to cooperate and not make a big deal out of it. But I held a grudge against this professor for a long time. I didn't understand why he was trying to make my life and my seminary experience so miserable. I didn't understand why, and to be honest, I still don't.

This is the guy Jesus wants me to pray for?

You may have enemies in your life. Some of them may be much more serious than what I just described. And you may wonder, "Why does Jesus want me to pray for my enemies?"

In Christ, we are not to be people of vengeance and bitterness. We are to be people of forgiveness. When you hold grudges or seek revenge, you are not acting like Christ. I'm not saying it's easy, or that you won't have to wrestle with things, but ultimately God wants us to have a heart of forgiveness. And if you can pray for your enemies, you are on the right path.

Time and time again Jesus prayed for His enemies. He even offered a prayer at His crucifixion: "Father, forgive them, for they do not know what they are doing." In the midst of death and betrayal, Jesus still prayed for His enemies. That's amazing! And if you don't think it's possible for us to

DEVOTIONAL

do the same, take a look at the apostle Stephen. His story is found in Acts, chapters 6 and 7. After Stephen testifies of Jesus' love and grace for the world, the crowd stones him to death. Before he dies, he falls on his knees and says, "Lord, do not hold this sin against them."

I know it's hard to pray for your enemies. You will need the strength and power of the Holy Spirit to be able to do it. If you are having a hard time with this, invite the Holy Spirit into your heart today!

IN CHRIST, WE ARE NOT TO BE PEOPLE OF VENGEANCE AND BITTERNESS.

Notice in this passage how Stephen, just like Jesus, had the power to pray for his enemies in the midst of dying.

ACTS 7:54–60

54 When the members of the Sanhedrin heard this, they were furious and gnashed their teeth at him. 55 But Stephen, full of the Holy Spirit, looked up to heaven and saw the glory of God, and Jesus standing at the right hand of God.

56 "Look," he said, "I see heaven open and the Son of Man standing at the right hand of God."

57 At this they covered their ears and, yelling at the top of their voices, they all rushed at him, 58 dragged him out of the city and began to stone him. Meanwhile, the witnesses laid their coats at the feet of a young man named Saul.

59 While they were stoning him, Stephen prayed, "Lord Jesus, receive my spirit." 60 Then he fell on his knees and cried out, "Lord, do not hold this sin against them." When he had said this, he fell asleep.

PRAY FOR THOSE WHO HAVE HURT YOU,

Abused you, or become your enemies. This isn't easy to do, but God will use it to transform your heart.

18/40

DAY 19

In this week of forgiveness, we've had the courage to recognize that we are sinful, we've dropped our rocks of judgment, we've forgiven ourselves, we've forgiven others, and we've even prayed for our enemies. There's been a real progression this week, and it all leads us to our quote for today: "Go now and leave your life of sin."

Earlier this week we heard the story of the adulterous woman who Jesus forgave. After He had forgiven her and set her free, He then pleaded with her to leave her life of sin.

God loves you for who you are, but He loves you too much to let you stay the way you are. I believe that when we encounter God and His grace, we are not to stay the same. The more we are with Jesus, the more we should want to become like Him and leave our former lives.

There's an amazing story about how God's grace and forgiveness changed an unlikely person, a tax collector named Zacchaeus. To finish our devotion for the day, let's first read his story:

GOD LOVES YOU FOR WHO YOU ARE, BUT HE LOVES YOU TOO MUCH TO LET YOU STAY THE WAY YOU ARE.

#REDLETTERCHALLENGE

LUKE 19:1–10

Jesus entered Jericho and was passing through. 2 A man was there by the name of Zacchaeus; he was a chief tax collector and was wealthy. 3 He wanted to see who Jesus was, but because he was short he could not see over the crowd. 4 So he ran ahead and climbed a sycamore-fig tree to see him, since Jesus was coming that way.

5 When Jesus reached the spot, he looked up and said to him, "Zacchaeus, come down immediately. I must stay at your house today." 6 So he came down at once and welcomed him gladly.

7 All the people saw this and began to mutter, "He has gone to be the guest of a sinner."

8 But Zacchaeus stood up and said to the Lord, "Look, Lord! Here and now I give half of my possessions to the poor, and if I have cheated anybody out of anything, I will pay back four times the amount."

9 Jesus said to him, "Today salvation has come to this house, because this man, too, is a son of Abraham. 10 For the Son of Man came to seek and to save the lost."

If you've grown up in the church, you've probably heard the song lyric, "Zacchaeus was a wee little man and a wee little man was he. He climbed up in the sycamore tree for the Lord he wanted to see..." Because Zacchaeus was "a wee little man," many of us underestimate his influence and power.

Tax collectors were some of the most hated people around because they were crooks and traitors. They were crooks because they made their money by collecting more in taxes than was due and keeping it. Most of them were rich. They were traitors because their country was under foreign occupation and they were working for the occupiers. They were despised and hated by those around them, and we can understand why.

Zacchaeus was not just a regular tax collector – he was a chief tax collector, so he had a team of tax collectors and he took a percentage of all of the money they made by cheating others. Zacchaeus was at the top of this large Ponzi scheme. He was the Bernie Madoff of Jesus's day. Over many years, he had bankrupted many people and made many enemies. He was most likely the richest of the rich, and everybody knew Zacchaeus.

But for whatever reason, Zacchaeus wants to see Jesus. And even more importantly, Jesus wants to meet Zacchaeus. When they meet, Jesus immediately befriends Zacchaeus and welcomes Him into relationship. What I love about this story is how immediate Zacchaeus' life change is.

When the grace of Jesus comes into your life, it prompts change. God doesn't want you to wait on the sidelines warming the bench. He wants you in the game. Jesus doesn't force Zacchaeus to change, but immediately Zacchaeus decides he's going to give half of his possessions to the poor and repay anyone he has wronged four times the amount. That's some serious restitution!

Here was a man idolizing money and power and taking advantage of his neighbors. But when Jesus calls out to Zacchaeus, his life is changed forever.

Zacchaeus didn't do this to be accepted by God; he didn't do it to be loved by God. He did it because he had been accepted and loved and forgiven by God. When a person sincerely moves what's in his head to his heart, it changes him. It's not business as usual. True repentance says I once beat prisoners, but now I tenderly care for those wounds. True repentance says I once used to cheat people financially, and now I repay them back with interest. True repentance says I used to deceive in business, but now I live with integrity. True repentance says I used to not take my marriage vows seriously, but now it's 'til death do us part.

After God invades your life, I pray you will never be the same. I pray you will not struggle with the sins of your past, and that instead God can use your pain to be your platform. That's why most people who are in recovery ministry today at one point struggled with addiction in the past. Most therapists went through therapy. If you are struggling with a particular sin, God has given you the forgiveness for it and the power to overcome it. My prayer is that you will leave that life of sin and allow God to use you to help someone else.

IF YOU ARE STRUGGLING WITH A PARTICULAR SIN,

Write down how you will overcome it and how you can help others who may be struggling with a similar sin.

_____

_____

_____

_____

_____

_____

_____

_____

19/40

WEEK OF

SER

VING

"FOR WE ARE GOD'S HANDIWORK,
CREATED IN CHRIST JESUS TO DO
GOOD WORKS, WHICH GOD PREPARED
IN ADVANCE FOR US TO DO."

EPHESIANS 2:10

DAY 20

"Because I said so!" How many of us remember those words from our parents? It's one of those statements you hate to hear when you're a kid! On the flip side, as a parent, you love this phrase because there is no great comeback for it. My wife and I use this one quite a bit these days because we have a five-year old, and five-year old's ask a ton of questions. Sometimes, if you actually indulge the question trail, you will get to some point where you will not know the answer and be forced to say, "Because I said so."

Today I want to talk about the motivation behind why we are embarking on this journey together. So far we've spent a week being with Christ and a week understanding how Christ has forgiven us and how we are to forgive others. Now, as we turn to a week of serving, there's going to be a lot of "doing." And I want to remind you that it's not because God says, "Do this" and "Do that" that we enter into a Challenge like this. A relationship with God is not about checking off a box that says "I did this," and "I did that" and "Look at how great I am." My relationship with God is all about receiving God's love and grace and being so compelled by that love and grace that I can't help but want to do what God is asking me to do!

We don't grit our teeth together and stomp our feet and say, "Fine, I'll do what God wants me to do." No, we do what God wants us to do because we love Him and we believe that following Him will lead us to eternal life!

The more we do what He is asking us to do, the more we find the abundant life we were made for. In fact, the entire motivation behind the Red Letter Challenge stems from the fact that God loved me first and **I am so overwhelmed by His love that I want to do something about it!**

Has anyone ever done something so great for you that you can't help but want to repay them?

Our actions flow from our heart.

Your actions do matter. That's why James, the brother of Jesus, said, "Faith without works is useless." It's one thing to say "I love you," but another thing to back it up by showing it.

In Matthew 22:36-39, a lawyer asked Jesus, *"What is the greatest command-ment to follow?" Jesus replied: 'Love the Lord your God with all your heart and with all your soul and with all your mind. This is the first and greatest commandment. And the second is like it: 'Love your neighbor as yourself.'"*

Ultimately we follow Jesus and His commandments because we love God and we want others to receive that love, too. When we love one another, others can actually see God in and through us. Jesus said in John 13:35: "By this everyone will know that you are my disciples, if you love one another."
All of the commandments and everything we will do in this Challenge come back to love, because through our love, others can be led to believe in Jesus. We don't do this Challenge because Jesus tells us we have to. We do this Challenge because God wants us to. He asks us to.

I heard Bill Hybels, pastor of Willow Creek Community Church, preach on the acronym "BYSSIW." It stands for, "Because you say so, I will." This is the phrase the disciple Peter echoed when Jesus asked him to cast out his nets into the deep water even though they'd already been fishing for hours with no luck. I'm sure Peter didn't really want to do this. But because the request came from Jesus, a man that Peter trusted, Peter was led to say, "Because you say so, I will."

And that's the key. All of these Challenges come directly out of the Bible. They are God's words to us today. And because they are God's words and because we love Him, may we adopt a "BYSSIW" attitude. Even when it is hard. Even when we do not understand why. Even when it is uncomfortable. BYSSIW!

BYSSIW: BECAUSE YOU SAY SO I WILL.

Today we're looking at the story behind the "BYSSIW" response of Simon Peter. He was a fisherman and had been fishing all night and hadn't caught anything. And Jesus, a carpenter by trade, gives him fishing advice. How would you have responded if you were Peter?

LUKE 5:4-11

4 When he had finished speaking, he said to Simon, "Put out into deep water, and let down the nets for a catch."

5 Simon answered, "Master, we've worked hard all night and haven't caught anything. But **because you say so, I will** let down the nets."

6 When they had done so, they caught such a large number of fish that their nets began to break.

7 So they signaled their partners in the other boat to come and help them, and they came and filled both boats so full that they began to sink.

8 When Simon Peter saw this, he fell at Jesus' knees and said, "Go away from me, Lord; I am a sinful man!" 9 For he and all his companions were astonished at the catch of fish they had taken, 10 and so were James and John, the sons of Zebedee, Simon's partners.

Then Jesus said to Simon, "Don't be afraid; from now on you will fish for people." 11 So they pulled their boats up on shore, left everything and followed him.

PRAY FOR A "BYSSIW" ATTITUDE FOR THIS CHALLENGE!

Leave sticky notes all over the house with the acronym "BYSSIW" to remember this Challenge throughout the day!

DAY 21

IF ANYONE WOULD BE FIRST, HE MUST
BE LAST OF ALL AND SERVANT TO ALL
MARK 9:35

Put yourself in my shoes. You're on a 5th grade retreat at church with some of your friends. Dinner's over and dessert time is just around the corner. You know that for dessert tonight it's going to be ice cream sandwiches, something you just love with a passion. In order to avoid total chaos, the youth pastor suggests that everyone come up alphabetically, one by one, to get their ice cream sandwich. This doesn't really sound fun or fair to you since your last name starts with a "Z." So finally, after Thomson, Weber, and Younghouse get their ice cream sandwiches, it's your turn. Up you go, only to hear the lady on the other side of the counter say as nicely as she can, "I'm sorry, but we just ran out. Looks like we were one short." Oh, the heartbreak. Can't you feel it? Isn't it rough being in my shoes?

Stay in them, because the next night you hear rumors they brought back the ice cream sandwiches for dessert again! Finally, I think, I'll get my ice cream sandwich and all peace on Earth can be restored again! In fact, I'm going to ask for two since I got ripped off yesterday. So, again in order to maintain a little peace at the campsite, the youth pastor lines everyone up, but this time he switches it so line up alphabetically by first name. Oh, great! Again, back of the line. Finally, after Tom and Will get their desserts, it's your turn. You approach the same lady again holding out your hands and just as you are getting ready to ask for two, she says, "Oh Zach, I'm so sorry, but it looks like we're just one short again. Next year I'll make a request to get more." Next year? I won't even be here next year! No one who is reading this knows what it's like to live as a Double Z. It's brutal! You get the last pick of everything, you get shafted on desserts, and you get chosen last on numerous occasions.

That's why this quotation of Jesus is my favorite of all! Because finally, I'll be first! I hope you know I'm kidding (sort of!). Jesus is calling us to put ourselves last and not first. This is not at all what we hear in our world today. We are taught to promote ourselves and to put our own needs first. We are taught to take care of ourselves and look out for "Number One." But Jesus tells us the opposite. **In Jesus' counter-cultural Kingdom, the ones who are blessed are the ones who serve others and put others before themselves.** Time and time again, Jesus talks about being a servant, practicing humility, being meek, and doing things for others. Jesus didn't just talk about serving others, He did it.

Some of my favorite verses depicting Christ as a servant are found in Philippians 2:5-11, which says:

> *In your relationships with one another, have the same mindset as Christ*
>
> *Jesus: Who, being in very nature God, did not consider equality with*
>
> *God something to be used to his own advantage; rather, he made*
>
> *himself nothing by taking the very nature of a servant, being made in*
>
> *human likeness. And being found in appearance as a man, he humbled*

himself by becoming obedient to death — even death on a cross!

Therefore God exalted him to the highest place and gave him the name

that is above every name, that at the name of Jesus every knee should

bow, in heaven and on earth and under the earth, and every tongue

acknowledge that Jesus Christ is Lord, to the glory of God the Father.

We will be doing a lot of serving this week. Perhaps nothing connects us more to the ministry of Christ than when we go out and serve.

IN JESUS' COUNTER-CULTURAL KINGDOM, THE ONES WHO ARE BLESSED ARE THE ONES WHO SERVE OTHERS AND PUT OTHERS BEFORE THEMSELVES.

One of the greatest examples of servants from the Bible was the cousin of Jesus, named John the Baptist. He came with a very clear instruction to "Prepare the way for the Lord." He became very popular and people came from far and wide to see him. But rather than letting success get the best of him, he always pointed to Jesus.

JOHN 3:22-30

22 After this, Jesus and his disciples went out into the Judean countryside, where he spent some time with them, and baptized. 23 Now John also was baptizing at Aenon near Salim, because there was plenty of water, and people were coming and being baptized. 24 (This was before John was put in prison.) 25 An argument developed between some of John's disciples and a certain Jew over the matter of ceremonial washing. 26 They came to John and said to him, "Rabbi, that man who was with you on the other side of the Jordan—the one you testified about—look, he is baptizing, and everyone is going to him."

27 To this John replied, "A person can receive only what is given them from heaven. 28 You yourselves can testify that I said, 'I am not the Messiah but am sent ahead of him.' 29 The bride belongs to the bridegroom. The friend who attends the bridegroom waits and listens for him, and is full of joy when he hears the bridegroom's voice. That joy is mine, and it is now complete. 30 He must become greater; I must become less."

FIND A WAY TO PUT SOMEONE ELSE'S NEEDS BEFORE YOURS TODAY.

21/40

DAY 22

WHEN YOU GIVE A DINNER, INVITE
THE POOR, CRIPPLED, LAME, ETC.
LUKE 14:13

The context of our passages today is from Luke 14:12-14 :

Then Jesus said to his host, "When you give a luncheon or dinner, do not invite your friends, your brothers or sisters, your relatives, or your rich neighbors; if you do, they may invite you back and so you will be repaid. But when you give a banquet, invite the poor, the crippled, the lame, the blind, and you will be blessed. Although they cannot repay you, you will be repaid at the resurrection of the righteous."

Today I want to focus on the people God calls us to serve. It's really easy to serve your good friends or family. It's really easy to serve those people in your life who are well-connected and could help you be more successful. It's a lot harder to serve those who may not ever be able to offer you anything.

My wife's family regularly invites people who have no family around to join them on holidays. Many times for the 4th of July or Easter or Thanksgiving they'll invite some foreign exchange students to eat and celebrate with them. I really respect them for doing this. (I'm not just writing that because I know they'll read this and I'll get brownie points, though that is kind of a nice bonus.) I respect this because most likely they will not get anything in return from many of the folks they invite.

Many times we serve and expect to receive something in return. But God wants us to be people who just naturally serve and don't expect anything back in this world. He tells us not to worry about the rewards we will get back right now, but instead He says we will be repaid when Christ returns.

It's really hard to wait though, isn't it? All of us have been spoiled with the, "I want it now, gotta have it now" mentality. If you're a good friend and I send you a text, I expect to see bubbles relatively quickly on my phone. I want to know you're texting me back quickly. If I'm streaming a video on Netflix, I don't want it to buffer, I want it now. If I'm watching my favorite show, I don't want to wait until next week for the next episode – I want to binge watch the whole season. If I'm ordering something on my phone on Amazon, I want free shipping and I want it in two days. It would be even better if it could be here now. At Virginia Tech, you can order Chipotle from your dorm room and it will be delivered by a drone in less than 30 minutes How cool is that?

We've been so conditioned to want things now that it's really difficult for so many people to actually think about tomorrow. It's hard to imagine rewards that will be waiting for us in heaven. We want everything now, including our rewards!

What's amazing about Jesus is that the people He came to serve would continually let Him down. Jesus didn't wait for us to have everything together before He served us. Instead, He gave His life for us while we were still a mess. Romans 5:8 says, "But **God demonstrates his own love for us in this: While we were still sinners, Christ died for us.**"

I do not deserve what Christ has done for me. **Jesus has served me and I am not worthy of being served.** I continually let Him down with my thoughts, words, and deeds. And yet, He serves me.

When I find it hard to serve people who won't help me get ahead in this world, I remember that Jesus stooped down low to save me. He doesn't need me for anything. I can't help Him climb any corporate ladder. He doesn't need my connections. He's not going to turn to me for help in a financial crisis.

It's important that we remember that we do not serve in order to get something. **We serve because we want to be more like Jesus.**

WE SERVE BECAUSE WE WANT TO BE MORE LIKE JESUS.

In this story, Jesus is having dinner before His crucifixion. The night before He would give His life, Jesus serves His disciples by washing their feet. What's amazing is He even washes the feet of Judas Iscariot, the disciple who would betray Him. Jesus proves we don't just serve those we will one day benefit from, but also those we don't expect anything from. We pick up the story as Jesus washes the feet of Simon Peter.

JOHN 13:6-17

6 He came to Simon Peter, who said to him, "Lord, are you going to wash my feet?"

7 Jesus replied, "You do not realize now what I am doing, but later you will understand."

8 "No," said Peter, "you shall never wash my feet."
Jesus answered, "Unless I wash you, you have no part with me."
9 "Then, Lord," Simon Peter replied, "not just my feet but my hands and my head as well!"

10 Jesus answered, "Those who have had a bath need only to wash their feet; their whole body is clean. And you are clean, though not every one of you." 11 For he knew who was going to betray him, and that was why he said not every one was clean.

12 When he had finished washing their feet, he put on his clothes and returned to his place. "Do you understand what I have done for you?" he asked them. 13 "You call me 'Teacher' and 'Lord,' and rightly so, for that is what I am. 14 Now that I, your Lord and Teacher, have washed your feet, you also should wash one another's feet. 15 I have set you an example that you should do as I have done for you. 16 Very truly I tell you, no servant is greater than his master, nor is a messenger greater than the one who sent him. 17 Now that you know these things, you will be blessed if you do them.

THE CHALLENGE TODAY IS TO SERVE SOMEONE WHO WILL NOT BE ABLE TO GIVE YOU ANYTHING IN RETURN.

Maybe you will take Jesus' words literally and host a meal for a group of people who could really use a nice meal. If that's too uncomfortable, perhaps you could team up with your small group or folks from your church and offer a free meal in your community at a local park.

22/40

DAY 23

Let's be honest: there are some weird and frustrating neighbors out there.
Some are too loud, some are too dirty, some let their yards go, some let their
kids go crazy, some have way too many cats for our liking, and some even
steal our Internet signals!

When Jesus says, "Love your neighbor as yourself" the natural question to ask
is "Who is our neighbor?" A Jewish expert in the law asked Jesus that exact
question. He wanted to know who was considered his neighbor so he knew
who he had to help and who he didn't have to help.

Jesus went on to tell this story called the Good Samaritan of a man who was
stripped, beaten, and laid on the side of the road, all bloodied up and in need
of help. Two so-called righteous people (who would be considered priests or
pastors today) pass by this man and do nothing. Then a third man passed by.
He is a Samaritan man, which means he was from the rival town of the man
who was beaten up. He sees his rival in need and takes care of him. Jesus
was essentially telling us that anyone who is in need is our neighbor. Being a
"neighbor" doesn't have to mean the people you live right next to, though
they are also your neighbors. A neighbor is anyone you come into contact
with.

Let's face it…most of the time we don't walk on a road and see someone
bloodied up who needs our help. In fact, the most common example of a

modern-day "Good Samaritan" story might be helping someone who is on the side of the road when their car breaks down. I often feel guilty for driving past people in this situation, but the reality is that I would be one of the last people they would ever want to have stop, because I know nothing about cars! I essentially have nothing to offer them except for moral support and pastoral counseling on the frustrations of broken-down cars. Maybe I'm just trying to make myself feel okay about this situation, but I think what Jesus is trying to tell us is that if we see a neighbor in need and we really legitimately have the ability to help, then by all means, do all you can to help. Use your gifts and talents for the benefit of your neighbor.

We may complain about our neighbors, and sometimes it may be hard to love them. But God can look down on us and say the same thing. Sometimes He must think, "Why do these people act like this...they are messy, they don't listen, they have no regard for me, they are not taking care of the stuff I've given them." It has to be hard for Him to love us. God could have looked down at us and said, "I'm done with them." Instead, **God looked down upon us and said, "They need my help."** He loves us so much that He sent Jesus to die on the cross for us and to pay the price for the sins we commit! Through His death and resurrection all who believe in Him are given eternal life when they die, and eternal life now as we participate and work with Him in bringing His Kingdom to this world.

As we continue our week of serving, let us remember to serve those who are our neighbors.

This is the story of the Good Samaritan. In it Jesus tells us that all people are our neighbors and we are called to help anyone in need.

LUKE 10:25-37

25 On one occasion an expert in the law stood up to test Jesus. "Teacher," he asked, "what must I do to inherit eternal life?"

26 "What is written in the Law?" he replied. "How do you read it?"
27 He answered, "'Love the Lord your God with all your heart and with all your soul and with all your strength and with all your mind'; and, 'Love your neighbor as yourself.'"

28 "You have answered correctly," Jesus replied. "Do this and you will live."

29 But he wanted to justify himself, so he asked Jesus, "And who is my neighbor?"

30 In reply Jesus said: "A man was going down from Jerusalem to Jericho, when he was attacked by robbers. They stripped him of his clothes, beat him and went away, leaving him half

going down the same road, and when he saw the man, he passed by on the other side. 32 So too, a Levite, when he came to the place and saw him, passed by on the other side. 33 But a Samaritan, as he traveled, came where the man was; and when he saw him, he took pity on him. 34 He went to him and bandaged his wounds, pouring on oil and wine. Then he put the man on his own donkey, brought him to an inn and took care of him. 35 The next day he took out two denarii and gave them to the innkeeper. 'Look after him,' he said, 'and when I return, I will reimburse you for any extra expense you may have.'

36 "Which of these three do you think was a neighbor to the man who fell into the hands of robbers?"

37 The expert in the law replied, "The one who had mercy on him."

Jesus told him, "Go and do likewise."

DO SOMETHING FOR A NEIGHBOR OF YOURS. SHOW THEM YOU CARE. NO STRINGS ATTACHED.

23/40

DAY 24

LET THE LITTLE CHILDREN
COME TO ME
MATTHEW 19:14

In Matthew 19, people bring their children to Jesus so He might heal them. The disciples told the parents to back away and stop bringing the children close to Jesus. Here was Jesus' response: "Let the little children come to me and do not hinder them, for to such belongs the Kingdom of heaven." Just one chapter earlier Jesus said," I tell you the truth, unless you change and become like little children, you will never enter the kingdom of heaven."[29] Many times I've wondered, "What does Jesus mean when He tells us we must become like little children in order to enter into His Kingdom?" I've always thought it was more important to grow and mature and become adults, and now He's telling us the opposite?

I have two little boys, Nathan and Brady. Practically every day I look at them and ask, "Why would God want me to become like my two little boys? Is there something they do or something they have that I'm missing?" So let's take a look at their lives and notice some things about them. They are very demanding. Often they're quite fussy. They're rather selfish, they don't share well, and they whine and complain frequently. In addition, they don't understand nearly as much as I do. They don't really contribute to society all that much yet, they aren't paying any bills, and they make huge messes wherever they go and expect someone else to pick up the pieces. They have no concept of the future and are only focused on the present. They can't take care of themselves and are completely dependent on others. I do love them, by the way! But why in the world would God tell me to become like them to enter into His Kingdom?

There's one other thing I notice about them, and I think this is what Jesus is getting at: they both have very sensitive spirits. They both feel really bad when they've done something wrong. They are genuinely sorry and they know they've messed up. And that's where God wants us: to be genuinely sorry and repentant. He wants us to acknowledge that we're imperfect, because **when we acknowledge we are imperfect, we are then open to receiving Christ's grace, which makes us perfect.**

This echoes the very first Beatitude in Matthew 5 where Jesus says, "Blessed are the poor in spirit, for theirs is the kingdom of heaven." The reality is the same here: the poor in spirit recognize they aren't perfect, feel genuinely sorry for it, and receive the grace of Jesus Christ to make them perfect. Children are really good examples of how to be poor in spirit and so in this way they are a model for us.

You might wonder how this devotion fits into our week of serving. So far we have talked about putting others' needs before ours, we've talked about serving those who won't be able to help us, and we've served our neighbors. Time and time again in His ministry, Jesus mentions how important children are. It's important that as we are doing the Red Letter Challenge, we invite our children to come along with us. The principles we are learning and the themes we are putting into practice are things every child should know. We have a responsibility to model to our children what God's love looks like.

In this story, you have a Pharisee who lived a good life and looked good on the outside. Then you have a tax collector, who was a failure according to this world's standards but was sorry for the life he had lived. Which one are you? Which one resembles how a child would feel? Which one is poor in spirit?

LUKE 18:9-14

9 To some who were confident of their own righteousness and looked down on everyone else, Jesus told this parable: 10 "Two men went up to the temple to pray, one a Pharisee and the other a tax collector. 11 The Pharisee stood by himself and prayed: 'God, I thank you that I am not like other people—robbers, evildoers, adulterers—or even like this tax collector. 12 I fast twice a week and give a tenth of all I get.'

13 "But the tax collector stood at a distance. He would not even look up to heaven, but beat his breast and said, 'God, have mercy on me, a sinner.'

14 "I tell you that this man, rather than the other, went home justified before God. For all those who exalt themselves will be humbled, and those

SERVE A CHILD WHO IS IN YOUR LIFE TODAY,

AND LET THIS CHILD KNOW HOW IMPORTANT HE OR SHE IS TO YOU.

_____

_____

_____

_____

_____

_____

_____

24/40

DAY 25

hate being sick! It is awful. As a parent of two young boys, it seems like
someone is sick almost every other week in our house. As parents, the worst
s when you are both sick and your little kids are actually healthy. There are
not many things harder in this world than being really, really sick and having to
care and look after two boys who are wound-up and ready to have some fun.

A lot of people have done a lot of great things for me in my life, but when
someone does something for me while I'm sick it feels even more special. One
of the greatest things anyone has ever done for me and my wife was when
our friend came and took our two boys to the mall for the afternoon when we
were both sick! Other people have taken our boys for an afternoon before, but
this particular time was so incredible because we were so sick.

t's hard to be sick. When you are sick, it feels good to be taken care of and to
receive encouragement from others. Many times throughout the Bible, Jesus
tells us how important it is to care for those who are sick or under-privileged.
One of the ways hurting and sick people know you care about them is when
you take time out of your day to show them you are thinking of them. You can
do many things to care for someone who is sick: visit, provide a meal, give
encouragement, give a gift, and pray.

Today's devotion is very simple: not to neglect or forget the sick, but to care
for them. When I'm healthy it's easy for me to forget that others may not be.

Others could be in pain, hurting, and in need of healing and encouragement. We have to be there for those people at all times!

There's a story in the Bible about a man who was paralyzed. The man had four friends and these four friends carried him on a mat all the way to see Jesus. When they got to the house where Jesus was, they saw the whole house was full of people. Rather than give up, they took their friend all the way to the top of the roof and lowered him through a hole so he could see Jesus. When Jesus saw the faith of the friends He forgave the paralyzed man and then He healed him. I've always thought it was amazing that it wasn't the faith of the paralyzed man that made him better; it was the faith of his friends.

Listen, I don't know how or why God heals some and not others. It seems like He heals some who have faith and others who have no faith. But here's what I do know: the friends of the paralyzed man had faith in Jesus and their friend was rewarded because of their faith. This means that **God honors your faith and your commitment to those in need**. I'm not saying God will always do something miraculous when you help someone in need, but He can and He has in the past.

Who do you know who is sick? Who do you know who needs encouragement? Being sick is not what we were meant for! We are looking forward to a time when Jesus promises us no more sickness, disease, death, or even tears! Jesus promises that all who follow Him will experience this sort of life. But until then, we have a responsibility to serve and take care of those who are sick.

In this story, we see four friends take care of their friend who was sick! What an incredible example of how to care for someone in need and look, in verse 5 below, at how Jesus responds not to the faith of the paralyzed man, but instead the faith of the friends!

MARK 2:1-12

A few days later, when Jesus again entered Capernaum, the people heard that he had come home. 2 They gathered in such large numbers that there was no room left, not even outside the door, and he preached the word to them. 3 Some men came, bringing to him a paralyzed man, carried by four of them. 4 Since they could not get him to Jesus because of the crowd, they made an opening in the roof above Jesus by digging through it and then lowered the mat the man was lying on. 5 When Jesus saw their faith, he said to the paralyzed man, "Son, your sins are forgiven."

6 Now some teachers of the law were sitting there, thinking to themselves, 7 "Why does this fellow talk like that? He's blaspheming! Who can forgive sins but God alone?"

8 Immediately Jesus knew in his spirit that this was what they were thinking in their hearts, and he said to them, "Why are you thinking these things? 9 Which is easier: to say to this paralyzed man, 'Your sins are forgiven,' or to say, 'Get up, take your mat and walk'? 10 But I want you to know that the Son of Man has authority on earth to forgive sins." So he said to the man, 11 "I tell you, get up, take your mat and go home." 12 He got up, took his mat and walked out in full view of them all. This amazed everyone and they praised God, saying, "We have never seen anything like this!"

IF YOU KNOW SOMEONE SICK, VISIT THAT PERSON.

Encourage, support, or call him/her. If you can't do that, then send a gift or message to someone you know who is sick. Lastly, if you don't know anyone personally who is sick, write encouraging "Get Well" cards and drop them off at a hospital.

25/40

DAY 26

It's important for us to not just talk about doing good things and meeting needs in the community, but to actually do them. It's how we show the rest of the world who God is! Take a look at what Jesus says in Matthew 5:13-16:

"You are the salt of the earth. But if the salt loses its saltiness, how can it be made salty again? It is no longer good for anything, except to be thrown out and trampled underfoot. "You are the light of the world. A town built on a hill cannot be hidden. Neither do people light a lamp and put it under a bowl. Instead they put it on its stand, and it gives light to everyone in the house. In the same way, let your light shine before others, that they may see your good deeds and glorify your Father in heaven.

In *The Journal of Biblical Counseling*, Timothy Keller makes the following observation about salt:

"The job of salt was to make something taste good. I don't know about you, but I can't stand corn on the cob without salt on it. When I have eaten a piece of corn on the cob that I really like, I put it down, and what do I say? 'That was great salt.' No, I say, 'That was great corn on the cob.' Why? Because the job of the salt is not to make you think how great the salt is, but how great the thing is with which it's involved."[30]

Jesus is calling you salt. As salt, our job is to go out and show people how great our God is. Every time I preach, the success of the sermon is not based on what people think of me. It's based on if I preached about Jesus and how He is our hero. If I preach and someone walks away from the sermon and all they can say about it was, "That pastor was smart," or "That pastor was funny," then I haven't done my job. My job is to point people to Jesus and give all glory to Him, not to myself. That's what salt does.

For this Challenge, your job as salt of the earth is to point people to God and show them how great our God is. That's really what it means for us to let our lights shine as well. Don't keep this light to yourself! By shining your light and being salt (in other words, by doing good works and meeting needs in the community) you show who God is to the rest of the world and ultimately fulfill what God has wanted all along for His people! God has wanted us to represent Him to the rest of the world from the beginning! This is what He wanted to do with the Israelites in the Old Testament; this is what He wanted for His disciples; and this is what He calls us, as His followers who make up the church, to do today. The amazing thing is that Jesus actually says that someone can see the good deeds we do and glorify God because of us! That's incredible!

However, I want to caution you on something I see quite often. It seems obvious but I need to point it out. I've seen a lot of Christians who shine their lights really bright in places that are already pretty well lit. In other words, I've seen a lot of people who believe in Jesus, do good works, and say all the right things about God in places where there are already many other Christians. It's easy to shine your light and serve in church or in a

Christian small group; it's very hard to shine your light in dark places or places where there are no Christians or where your viewpoints and opinions are not the majority. God calls us to shine our light not around other Christians, but especially in places where there is darkness.

It's amazing to think that **through what we do and the way we live, we can actually point people to a real relationship with God**. We may never know what kind of impact we have made in somebody else's life, but we will continue to be faithful in serving Him and giving Him the glory.

THROUGH WHAT WE DO AND THE WAY WE LIVE, WE CAN ACTUALLY POINT PEOPLE TO A REAL RELATIONSHIP WITH GOD.

Notice how similar these sections are to the section we read above in the devotion. God's plan from the beginning with the Israelites, the disciples of Jesus, and the church has always been that we would represent Him to the rest of the world by living a life of obedience and godliness.

EXODUS 19:3-6

3 Then Moses went up to God, and the Lord called to him from the mountain and said, "This is what you are to say to the descendants of Jacob and what you are to tell the people of Israel: 4 'You yourselves have seen what I did to Egypt, and how I carried you on eagles' wings and brought you to myself. 5 Now if you obey me fully and keep my covenant, then out of all nations you will be my treasured possession. Although the whole earth is mine, 6 you will be for me a kingdom of priests and a holy nation.' These are the words you are to speak to the Israelites."

1 PETER 2:9-12

9 But you are a chosen people, a royal priesthood, a holy nation, God's special possession, that you may declare the praises of him who called you out of darkness into his wonderful light. 10 Once you were not a people, but now you are the people of God; once you had not received mercy, but now you have received mercy.

11 Dear friends, I urge you, as foreigners and exiles, to abstain from sinful desires, which wage war against your soul. 12 Live such good lives among the pagans that, though they accuse you of doing wrong, they may see your good deeds and glorify God on the day he visits us.

SERVE GOD TODAY IN ONE OF THE FOLLOWING WAYS

- Organize a servant event with a local non-profit

- Volunteer at a food pantry or soup kitchen

- Volunteer with your local Habitat for Humanity

- Clean a neighbor's yard

- Visit an elderly person

- Encourage someone who is sick

_____

_____

_____

26/40

DAYS
27-33
OF THE ☀ 40 DAY
CHALLENGE

WEEK OF

GIVING

"IT IS MORE BLESSED TO GIVE
THAN TO RECEIVE."

ACTS 20:35

DAY 27

How many times have you truly given something and not received anything in return?

In their book *Super Freakonomics*, Stephen Levitt and Stephen Dubner write, "At *the University of Newcastle upon Tyne in England, a psychology professor named Melissa Bateson surreptitiously ran an experiment in her own department's break room. Customarily, faculty members paid for coffee and other drinks by dropping money into an 'honesty box.' Each week, Bateson posted a new price list. The prices never changed, but the small photograph atop the list did. On odd weeks, there was a picture of flowers; on even weeks, a pair of human eyes. When the eyes were watching, Bateson's colleagues left nearly three times as much money in the honesty box. So the next time you laugh when a bird is frightened off by a silly scarecrow, remember that scarecrows work on human beings too.*"[31]

It may appear altruistic when you donate $100 to your local public radio station, but in exchange you get a year of guilt-free listening (and, if you're lucky, a canvas tote bag). U.S. citizens are easily the world's leaders in per-capita charitable contributions, but the U.S. tax code is also among the most generous in allowing deductions for those contributions.

Economists say most giving is "impure altruism": You give not only because you want to help but because it makes you look good, or feel good, or perhaps feel less bad. You've done it before, and so have I. You don't have to feel bad if you do get something back in return. But I think the heart of what Jesus is saying is that the reason and **the attitude behind our giving should never be to get something in return.**

The reality is it's actually hard to give without getting something in return. Even our verse in Luke 6:35 says, "Lend without expecting to get anything back. Then your reward will be great, and you will be children of the Most High." Jesus tells us that when we give and expect nothing back, we will eventually get something back from God!

Ultimately **we worship a God who gave up His most prized possession for us!** He gave His very own Son, Jesus Christ, to die for us. Through His death and resurrection, He paid the entire price for all the sin we've ever committed and ever will commit. He didn't pay 99% of it and ask us to pay the last 1%. He paid it all.

As a follower of Jesus I know and believe in the reality of Jesus' death and resurrection. How disappointing it must be for God to look at me and see that I still fail Him. If He sent Jesus expecting that after His death and resurrection we would be eternally grateful and therefore live lives of complete holiness, He must be very disappointed. However, God sent Jesus not because He expected perfection from us, but simply because He loves us. However, God sent Jesus knowing that even after His death and resurrection we would fail Him.

That's what it means to lend, or give, without expecting in return.

We do not give because we have to. We give because we want to be like Jesus. We want to follow in the footsteps of our Savior who laid the foundation for us to give even when we may not get anything back in return.

I love this story because of its simplicity. There were no synagogues or places for the early Christians to meet in Philippi and so after being baptized Lydia offers her house to the church. She expects nothing in return. All she wants is to be a part of what God is doing in her city. She knew what the church needed; she knew she had it; and so she gave it to the church and her house became the headquarters for the church and mission work in Philippi.

ACTS 16:11-15

11 From Troas we put out to sea and sailed straight for Samothrace, and the next day we went on to Neapolis. 12 From there we traveled to Philippi, a Roman colony and the leading city of that district of Macedonia. And we stayed there several days.

13 On the Sabbath we went outside the city gate to the river, where we expected to find a place of prayer. We sat down and began to speak to the women who had gathered there. 14 One of those listening was a woman from the city of Thyatira named Lydia, a dealer in purple cloth. She was a worshiper of God. The Lord opened her heart to respond to Paul's message. 15 When she and the members of her household were baptized, she invited us to her home. "If you consider me a believer in the Lord," she said, "come and stay at my house." And she persuaded us.

AS WE START OUR WEEK OF GIVING, LEND OR GIVE TO SOMEONE AND DON'T ASK FOR OR EXPECT ANYTHING IN RETURN.

27/40

DAY 28

"Someone else will take care of that." How many times have we said that? When we hear about problems, sometimes our first response isn't "How can we help?" but rather, "Someone else will help."

Today's quotation from Jesus tells us it's not about someone else taking care of anything. God is telling us it is our job to feed the hungry. He is calling His followers to take care of things themselves. "That's somebody else's problem" is not in the vocabulary of Jesus or His followers. The truth is we all have gifts or talents or possessions we can offer to the world around us.

I love this story from Peter Sagal:

When Morgan was a young woman living in New York City, she had trouble finding herself. She was very uncertain of herself and she had become obsessed with Mother Teresa.

For some reason, Morgan thought Mother Teresa was the epitome of what a human being should be. One day Morgan found out Mother Teresa was coming to New York and she found out where she was staying. So Morgan parked on a curb outside the hotel, hoping to get a glimpse of her, when a car pulled up and Mother Teresa got out.

Morgan ran up to Mother Teresa and said, "I'm so glad to meet you. The work you do is so important and I want to come to Calcutta and work with you." Mother Teresa shook her head and said, "No, you don't do this work because you think it's good. You do this work because you so love the poor people of Calcutta that you can't be away from them. That's when you come and do this work." Morgan realized she had been busted a little bit (in a nice way).

Mother Teresa said, "What do you do?' Morgan said, "Nothing important. I work in a theater and help put on plays. What use is that?"

Mother Teresa replied, "There are many different kinds of famine in this world. In my country there is a famine of the body. In this country there is a famine of the spirit. Stay here and feed your people."[32]

All of us have something to offer. The God of the Universe, the one who has access to everything, invites us to be part of a miracle with Him. **God doesn't need us to participate in His miracles with Him, but He wants us to.**

Today's quote comes from the miraculous story of Jesus feeding 5000 people with only five loaves of bread and two fish. The crowds had been with Jesus all day and were hungry! The disciples wanted to send them home to get food when Jesus told them, "You give them something to eat." Can you imagine what they must have been thinking? "How are we going to feed them? This man is out of his mind!" Jesus was testing their faith.

Andy Stanley describes this story well:

"What do you do when Jesus is actually standing there telling you to do something you know you can't do? Apparently you do what we do. You make excuses and tell Him things He already knows...I'm not smart enough. I'm not educated enough. I'm not resourced enough. Get somebody else! But Jesus says, 'Just bring me what you do have and I'll work with that. Bring me your limited education, your lack of experience, along with your fear and insecurity, and watch what I can do'...if we, or the people in our churches, ever get to the place where we are willing to make what we have available to God, amazing things will happen."[33]

For whatever reason, God has chosen to work with us in redeeming and restoring this world. He's chosen us to be the people who speak and act on His behalf. God believes you can make a difference. That's why He's chosen you. 1 Corinthians 3:10 calls us "co-workers" or "co-laborers" with God. We have already been called by God to work with Him and given the tools to grow His Kingdom! Don't wait for permission from your pastor or someone else to do what God has put in your heart. God has called you and He's filled you up with the Holy Spirit to give you everything you need to make a difference in this world. You may feel like you don't have a lot to offer, but I want you to know that the same God that turned a boy's lunch into food for 5000 can do the same for you. **God can do a lot with a little.**

GOD CAN DO A LOT WITH A LITTLE.

This is the story of Jesus turning one boy's lunch into food for thousands. You may feel like you don't have a lot to offer, but I want you to know that the same God that multiplied a boy's lunch into food for 5000 can do the same with whatever you offer to Him.

MATTHEW 14:13-21

13 When Jesus heard what had happened, he withdrew by boat privately to a solitary place. Hearing of this, the crowds followed him on foot from the towns. 14 When Jesus landed and saw a large crowd, he had compassion on them and healed their sick.

15 As evening approached, the disciples came to him and said, "This is a remote place, and it's already getting late. Send the crowds away, so they can go to the villages and buy themselves some food."

16 Jesus replied, "They do not need to go away. You give them something to eat."
17 "We have here only five loaves of bread and two fish," they answered.

18 "Bring them here to me," he said. 19 And he directed the people to sit down on the grass. Taking the five loaves and the two fish and looking up to heaven, he gave thanks and broke the loaves. Then he gave them to the disciples, and the disciples gave them to the people. 20 They all ate and were satisfied, and the disciples picked up twelve basketfuls of broken pieces that were left over.

21 The number of those who ate was about five thousand men, besides women and children.

WHAT IS SOMETHING YOU OWN TODAY THAT COULD BENEFIT SOMEONE ELSE? POOL? LAWN MOWER? CARPET CLEANER? TRUCK?

_____

_____

_____

_____

_____

_____

28/40

DAY 29

We hear a lot about food in our country. We hear a lot about obesity and how much Americans eat. In fact, in 2011, the average American ate a ton of food (1996 pounds to be exact). That includes more than 630 pounds of dairy, 185 pounds of meat, 197 pounds of grains, almost 700 pounds of fruits and veggies, and more than 200 pounds of sweets and fats![34] Most of us don't have to worry about eating; we simply have to ask, "What are we going to eat today?" However, there are still millions of people in our country that are without food or are in need.

Yet Americans discard 40 percent of the food supply every year, and the average American family of four ends up throwing away an equivalent of up to $2,275 in food each year. Just a 15 percent reduction in losses in the U.S. food supply would save enough to feed 25 million Americans annually.[35] I can't blame everyone else on this one. My family suffers from this too and we've started to do something about it. We noticed our two boys barely eat half of what we give them. My wife I began to feel bad about this and started to serve ourselves less because we realized we would get full just by eating their leftovers and we could then throw less food away.

Jesus was talking to a large group of people when He drops this bomb on them:

"'For I was hungry and you gave me something to eat, I was thirsty and you gave me something to drink, I was a stranger and you invited me in, I needed clothes and you clothed me, I was sick and you looked after me, I

was in prison and you came to visit me.'

"Then the righteous will answer him, 'Lord, when did we see you hungry and feed you, or thirsty and give you something to drink? When did we see you a stranger and invite you in, or needing clothes and clothe you? When did we see you sick or in prison and go to visit you?'

"The King will reply, 'Truly I tell you, whatever you did for one of the least of these brothers and sisters of mine, you did for me.'"[36]

We've learned in this Challenge that one of the ways people will see God in us is when we actually do what He says to do. Here Jesus says that whatever we do for the least of those in the world, the least privileged, we've done it for Him. He says that **the people who take care of the least privileged will be the ones who are welcomed into His Kingdom.** This isn't a scare tactic. Jesus isn't saying, "If you don't do this, then you'll burn in Hell." He's simply saying, "The people who believe in Jesus are the people who help the least privileged." That's just what they do! The stronger a person's relationship with God, the more natural it becomes to take care of God's children in this world.

My role on a board of directors for a food pantry here in Mount Dora, FL is a constant reminder to me that there are a countless number of people who are hungry. Even in America, the land of blessing and opportunity, people are still starving. They need help! Who better to help them than the followers of Jesus?

If your cupboards are full, if you don't have to worry about what you will eat or drink tomorrow because you know you will have plenty, then you can help in this cause.

In this Old Testament story, Elisha helps out a widow. All she has is one jar of olive oil but as we can see from this story, God can turn a little bit into a lot.

2 KINGS 4:1-7

GIVE FOOD TO THE NEEDY.

Whether it's giving it to someone on the side of the street or donating to your local food pantry, be generous. Clear out your cupboards or go shopping and collect food for the needy. You can either donate on your own or bring it to your local church to give to a food pantry.

SPEAKING OF THAT, if your local church doesn't have a food pantry box where people can donate food on a regular basis, tell your pastor you are going to bring one in!

29/40

DAY 30

"There once was a rich man who was near death. He was very grieved because he had worked so hard for his money and wanted to be able to take it with him to heaven. So he began to pray that he might be able to take some of his wealth with him.

An angel heard his plea and appeared to him. 'Sorry, but you can't take your wealth with you.'

The man begged the angel to speak to God to see if He might bend the rules. The man continued to pray that his wealth could follow him. The angel reappeared and informed the man that God had decided to allow him to take one suitcase with him.

Overjoyed, the man gathered his largest suitcase and filled it with pure gold bars and placed it beside his bed. Soon afterward, he died and showed up at the gates of heaven to greet St. Peter.

St. Peter, seeing the suitcase, said, 'Hold on, you can't bring that in here!' The man explained to St. Peter that he had permission and asked him to verify his story with the Lord. Sure enough, St. Peter checked it out, came back and said, 'You're right. You are allowed one carry-on bag, but I'm supposed to check its contents before letting it through.'

St. Peter opened the suitcase to inspect the worldly items that the man *found too precious to leave behind and exclaimed, 'You brought pavement?'"* [37]

Jesus talks in the Sermon on the Mount about making sure we don't store up treasures on earth, but instead store up treasures in heaven.

He mentions not worrying about clothes, and this is something I've never had to worry about. I feel guilty sometimes seeing all that I have and knowing others don't have as much. A couple of years ago, I posted something on Facebook about how many pairs of shoes my wife had. Out of everything I posted all year, this drummed up the most comments from my family and friends! I asked the question, "Should she give some away or is it okay for a woman to have this many pairs of shoes?" The responses were all over the map. She did end up giving away a lot of her shoes to charity and I was really proud of her for that. But now I'm wondering about myself – how many pairs of shoes do *I really* need?

Do I have too much? Or can someone else benefit from stuff that's just sitting around in my closets and dressers? What about you? How much is too much?

God says that **whenever we do something for the "least of these" in our world, or the least privileged, it's like we do it for Jesus.** Imagine Jesus on the side of the road with no clothes. If you knew it was Jesus what would you do? Of course you would clothe Him. You would give Him whatever He needed! If your dressers are full and you don't have to worry about whether or not you'll have clothes tomorrow, you can be a big part in completing today's Challenge!

Listen to Jesus' words about what it means to store up treasures in heaven as opposed to accumulating earthly things like clothes.

MATTHEW 6:19–21, 24–34

19 "Do not store up for yourselves treasures on earth, where moths and vermin destroy, and where thieves break in and steal. 20 But store up for yourselves treasures in heaven, where moths and vermin do not destroy, and where thieves do not break in and steal. 21 For where your treasure is, there your heart will be also.

24 "No one can serve two masters. Either you will hate the one and love the other, or you will be devoted to the one and despise the other. You cannot serve both God and money.

25 "Therefore I tell you, do not worry about your life, what you will eat or drink; or about your body, what you will wear. Is not life more than food, and the body more than clothes? 26 Look at the birds of the air; they do not sow or reap or store away in barns, and yet your heavenly Father feeds them. Are you not much more valuable than they? 27 Can any one of you by worrying add a single hour to your life?

28 "And why do you worry about clothes? See how the flowers of the field grow. They do not labor or spin. 29 Yet I tell you that not even Solomon in all his splendor was dressed like one of these. 30 If that is how God clothes the grass of the field, which is here today and tomorrow is thrown into the fire, will he not much more clothe you—you of little faith? 31 So do not worry, saying, 'What shall we eat?' or 'What shall we drink?' or 'What shall we wear?' 32 For the pagans run after all these things, and your heavenly Father knows that you need them. 33 But seek first his kingdom and his righteousness, and all these things will be given to you as well. 34 Therefore do not worry about tomorrow, for tomorrow will worry about itself. Each day has enough trouble of its own.

GO THROUGH YOUR DRESSERS AND CLOSETS AND GIVE ALL THE CLOTHES YOU DON'T NEED TO CHARITY.

30/40

DAY 31

Money is an extremely divisive topic, because **how you spend your money shows where your heart is.** Jesus said it: "For where your treasure is, there your heart is also."[38]

Whenever a Christian leader talks about money, it can cause negative reactions. In fact, one of the biggest reasons people leave a church or don't attend church is the church's emphasis on money.

I believe this is for two reasons. First, some think the church has no right to tell them what to do with money. They've seen the church use it in ways that haven't always honored God, so why should they give?

I was sickened by a television show called "Preachers of LA" which followed the lives of six preachers. I don't know any of the preachers or their families personally. I know that God can work through each of them, but it bothers me when I see preachers who have become tremendously rich. You can make any excuse you want, but that lifestyle doesn't look good on preachers, and I don't think it's what Jesus had in mind when He called us to follow Him. If my money was going to someone or something like that, I wouldn't want to give it away either.

But there's a second reason we don't like to talk about money: we really like our money. **Money is the number one idol in our lives.** It is really difficult to separate people from something they love so much.

Please understand there is nothing wrong with money in itself. It's not money that is the root of all evil, but the love of money.

Jesus tells the Pharisees not to neglect the tithe. A tithe is literally a tenth. If I make $100, $10 would be the tithe. I hear some people say, "I tithe 5%." But if you are giving 5%, that is an offering, not a tithe.

Jesus only said one thing about tithing in the four Gospels, in Matthew 23:23 (NLT) "What sorrow awaits you teachers of religious law and you Pharisees. Hypocrites! For you are careful to tithe even the tiniest income from your herb gardens, but you ignore the more important aspects of the law--justice, mercy, and faith. You should tithe, yes, but do not neglect the moro important things "

Jesus talked a lot about giving, but not much about tithing. Because of that, some pastors don't teach on the importance of tithing.

But the practice of tithing goes all the way back to Abraham. From the beginning, God's people have returned the first 10% to Him as an offering to show that we fully trust Him to provide for us.

If someone were to look into your bank account, would they know you are a follower of Jesus? **You cannot truly go all in for God if you cannot trust God with your money.** I believe in our nation tithing could possibly be the number one indicator of an abiding faith in Jesus Christ.

I haven't always felt this way. In fact, I've really struggled in this area. I remember the first time I had a considerable amount of extra money. Rather than buying something important, investing in my family's future, or giving to God, I gambled it away. I snuck behind my family's back to do it. I was studying to be a pastor, and I wasted thousands of dollars. I don't know which was a bigger issue: the competition of gambling or the greed of always wanting more, but I failed miserably and had to repent.

I have found out personally that God can give you complete victory in an area that was once a struggle. **He can redeem what was once broken and turn it into one of your biggest strengths.** Now when I take a spiritual gift test, one of my top three gifts is generosity. In fact, last year when I did my taxes online, my tax return showed a high risk of audit because my charitable contributions were way out of proportion with my income.

I'm proud of that. God has redeemed me and made me a generous person. And I'll tell you something else: I've never regretted giving any of the dollars to the church. And you never will either.

If 10% was required by the law, then **how much more should we give now that we operate out of God's grace?** I believe the tithe is the starting place, not the finish line. There are a lot of things to do to follow Jesus the way He wants us to, but follow Christ's command today: don't neglect the tithe!

YOU CANNOT TRULY GO ALL IN FOR GOD IF YOU CANNOT TRUST GOD WITH YOUR MONEY.

This is the only time in all of the Bible that God tells His followers to "Test him." Test Him with your tithe, and see how God will pour out His blessings on you. It doesn't always mean material blessing in this world, but when we give to God, we are always blessed.

MALACHI 3:6-12

6 *"I the Lord do not change. So you, the descendants of Jacob, are not destroyed. 7 Ever since the time of your ancestors you have turned away from my decrees and have not kept them. Return to me, and I will return to you," says the Lord Almighty.*

"But you ask, 'How are we to return?'

8 *"Will a mere mortal rob God? Yet you rob me.*

"But you ask, 'How are we robbing you?'

"In tithes and offerings. 9 You are under a curse—your whole nation— because you are robbing me. 10 Bring the whole tithe into the storehouse, that there may be food in my house. Test me in this," says the Lord Almighty, "and see if I will not throw open the floodgates of heaven and pour out so much blessing that there will not be room enough to store it. 11 I will prevent pests from devouring your crops, and the vines in your fields will not drop their fruit before it is ripe," says the Lord Almighty. 12 "Then all the nations will call you blessed, for yours will be a delightful land," says the Lord Almighty.

TITHE FOR THE NEXT 6 MONTHS TO YOUR LOCAL CHURCH.

If you don't have a local church to give your tithe to, I'll give you my church's website! Just kidding! In all seriousness, find a local church or charity that is making a difference and start giving sacrificially and watch how God works in big ways!

31/40

DAY 32

SELL ALL THAT YOU POSSESS AND GIVE TO THE POOR
MARK 10:21

America makes up less than 5% of the world's population, yet controls 20% of the world's wealth.

One billion people in the world do not have access to clean water, while the average American uses 400-600 liters of water a day.

Every seven seconds, somewhere in the world a child under age five dies of hunger, while Americans throw away 14% of the food we purchase.

40% of people in the world lack basic sanitation, while 49 million diapers are used and thrown away in America every day.

Americans spend more annually on trash bags than nearly half of the world does on all goods.[39]

While there are many that are struggling in our nation, the above statistics point out that the majority of us have plenty. By all accounts, as a nation, we are experiencing tremendous wealth. The more we dig into the words of Jesus and His action statements in the Gospels, the more we see how much the followers of Jesus are meant to be givers! But today's words from Jesus kick it up to a level we haven't seen yet. This one might be the hardest of all of the quotes we've looked at in the Challenge so far!

Whatever you invest in financially you will also connect to emotionally, as well. If you give money to a university, you will monitor how that university is doing. If you are a member of a country club, you will make sure they are keeping the golf course in great shape. I am part of a Homeowner's Association and because I pay dues to that every month I expect others to keep their houses and yards up to the required level.

Our emotions follow our money, so Jesus is telling you to invest in Him. Give to His Kingdom. Give to the church. Give to people who need help. Give to organizations that are meeting needs in the community.

I believe God asks us to give until it hurts until it feels good!

Giving should hurt. In other words, it should be a sacrifice. Yesterday we talked about tithing, but for some people giving a tithe is not really a sacrifice at all. They believe that because they are tithing they are doing what God wants them to do. But the reality is that if you make $1 million a year and you are giving $100,000 to your local church, that $100,000 will make a huge difference to the church but it's not a sacrifice for you. The sacrifice would be to give $900,000 and live on $100,000!

The more you start giving the easier it gets. It hurts to sacrifice at first, but if you keep giving and sacrificing, it begins to feel really good! The closest thing I can equate it to is exercising and working out. If you haven't worked out for a while and then all of a sudden go in and lift weights, you will be very sore, especially if you push yourself hard while you are there. But you will realize it's "good pain." Then you work out again and you feel less pain.

And then the next time, even less pain. This pattern continues until you work out and experience no pain at all.

The same is true of giving. **To follow after God faithfully means following after Him with everything you have**, including your money and your possessions. He wants you to be a generous person. If you haven't given in a while or if you've given but not sacrificially, then giving what God actually wants you to give will hurt. But it will feel good at the same time. Then you will give again, and it will still hurt, but it will hurt less. And as you keep giving, it will hurt less each time, until all of a sudden you are giving and it doesn't even hurt at all!

Today's quotation is so hard and so shocking that it forces us to ask the question: How serious is Jesus here? Does He really want us to sell everything and give it to the poor? What is everything? Like everything everything? Am I giving until it hurts until it feels good?

TO FOLLOW AFTER GOD FAITHFULLY MEANS FOLLOWING AFTER HIM WITH EVERYTHING YOU HAVE.

The man who asks Jesus how to inherit eternal life has lived a pretty good life according to the world's standards. But we see his heart was torn and leaned more towards earthly wealth than following after Jesus.

MARK 10:17-27

17 As Jesus started on his way, a man ran up to him and fell on his knees before him. "Good teacher," he asked, "what must I do to inherit eternal life?"

18 "Why do you call me good?" Jesus answered. "No one is good—except God alone. 19 You know the commandments: 'You shall not murder, you shall not commit adultery, you shall not steal, you shall not give false testimony, you shall not defraud, honor your father and mother.'"

20 "Teacher," he declared, "all these I have kept since I was a boy."
21 Jesus looked at him and loved him. "One thing you lack," he said. "Go, sell everything you have and give to the poor, and you will have treasure in heaven. Then come, follow me."

22 At this the man's face fell. He went away sad, because he had great wealth. 23 Jesus looked around and said to his disciples, "How hard it is for the rich to enter the kingdom of God!"

24 The disciples were amazed at his words. But Jesus said again, "Children, how hard it is to enter the kingdom of God! 25 It is easier for a camel to go through the eye of a needle than for someone who is rich to enter the kingdom of God."

26 The disciples were even more amazed, and said to each other, "Who then can be saved?"

27 Jesus looked at them and said, "With man this is impossible, but not with God; all things are possible with God."

GIVE SACRIFICIALLY TODAY. PRAY ABOUT WHERE TO GIVE AND HOW TO GIVE IT, THEN ACT IN FAITH.

_____

_____

_____

_____

_____

_____

32/40

DAY 33

IT IS BETTER TO GIVE
THAN RECEIVE
ACTS 20:35

Which is really better: to give or to receive?

I'll be honest with you; when I was younger I thought it was much better
to get things than to give them. At Christmas, I loved getting things and
really didn't care what others got. But now, in my old age, my thinking has
changed. Now I get much more satisfaction in giving a gift than in receiving
one. When I buy a gift for someone I truly care about, it's so hard to keep it
a secret!

My wife and I got married in 2004 and in December of that year we moved
away from Wisconsin to Missouri, leaving many friends we had met in
college. In Missouri we had no real friends and we were both several
hundred miles away from our families. Although we were far from family, I
still remembered the traditions my family had around holidays. In our family,
we stayed up late on Christmas Eve and opened gifts after my dad got
home from all of the Christmas Eve services. Because he was pastor of a
large church, there were multiple worship services and the last one didn't
start until 11PM, so dad didn't get home until about one in the morning.
Then we would open presents! I loved and cherished those moments.

So that Christmas in Missouri I bought my wife a pair of shoes I knew she
really wanted and she bought me a golf club that I really wanted. We were
both so excited to give each other the gifts we bought. And since we

weren't constricted to our old traditions anymore, we decided we couldn't wait any longer, and our first Christmas together we opened our gifts for each other on December 11th! The next year we did a little better; we made it until December 13th. Now we have kids and have to be responsible adults, so we're back to a normal Christmas Eve gift opening!

But here's the point in all of this: when you have a good gift for someone you care about, you can't wait to give it away.

Jordan Grafman actually asked the question,

> "Is it better to give or to receive?" According to an article on Sharpbrains.com, "He asked nineteen fit volunteers to participate in a computer game while having their brains scanned by an fMRI. An fMRI is a machine that scans the brain that measures increased blood flow to the different blood vessels that accompany brain usage. And through scanning the brain, they were actually able to tell in this game whether people got more excited about giving or receiving a gift. The way the game was played was it gave out cash rewards for doing well and offered the contestants a chance to either receive the reward or to donate and to give the reward to someone else. The team of scientists found that giving a present to another being actually feels better than receiving a gift from one."[40]

We have all been given the most amazing gift in the entire world by receiving the grace of Jesus Christ in our life. As amazing as it is to receive this gift, it is even better when we can give that gift to others. Any time I've ever gotten a gift I really like, I love to tell others about it. I'm sure you are the same way, too, yet so often we fail to give people this greatest gift!

The best thing you can do with a good gift is rip it open, enjoy it, and share it with others. I hope you think about this for your life. Are you sharing the greatest gift you've ever been given with someone else right now? If not, why not? If you are, isn't it amazing?

THE BEST THING
YOU CAN DO
WITH A GOOD
GIFT IS RIP IT
OPEN, ENJOY IT,
AND SHARE IT
WITH OTHERS.

The churches in Macedonia were excited to give even in the midst of their poverty. Pay special attention to the last verse; this is where all of our generosity stems from.

2 CORINTHIANS 8:1–10

And now, brothers and sisters, we want you to know about the grace that God has given the Macedonian churches. 2 In the midst of a very severe trial, their overflowing joy and their extreme poverty welled up in rich generosity. 3 For I testify that they gave as much as they were able, and even beyond their ability. Entirely on their own, 4 they urgently pleaded with us for the privilege of sharing in this service to the Lord's people. 5 And they exceeded our expectations: They gave themselves first of all to the Lord, and then by the will of God also to us. 6 So we urged Titus, just as he had earlier made a beginning, to bring also to completion this act of grace on your part. 7 But since you excel in everything—in faith, in speech, in knowledge, in complete earnestness and in the love we have kindled in you—see that you also excel in this grace of giving.

8 I am not commanding you, but I want to test the sincerity of your love by comparing it with the earnestness of others. 9 For you know the grace of our Lord Jesus Christ, that though he was rich, yet for your sake he became poor, so that you through his poverty might become rich.

GIVE A GREAT GIFT TO A WORTHY PERSON OR CHARITY TODAY!

_____

_____

_____

_____

_____

_____

_____

_____

33/40

DAYS
34-40

OF THE 40 DAY

CHALLENGE

WEEK OF

GOING

"THEREFORE GO AND
MAKE DISCIPLES
OF ALL NATIONS."

MATTHEW 28:19A

DAY 34

This may sound strange, but I find it difficult to pray with my wife. You would think that because I'm a pastor and we are both Christians that this would come naturally to us. But we don't pray together as often as we should. In fact, it's challenging for me to get into deep conversations about faith at home.

I think there are two reasons for this.

One is my job. I'm a pastor and so I get into these conversations all the time. Often the last thing I want to do when I get home is more of my job. I love God, but I want to relax, take a break from it, and turn on a ball game sometimes.

The second reason is myself. My family knows me better than anyone else. They see me as a pastor boldly declaring the Word of God and then they see me at home boldly failing to put it into practice. They see my failures and my faults, so how can I lead them into conversations about faith?

It is often hard to share God and the things He is doing in your life with your family. They know you better than anyone else, and so they are the first to know when you fail.

Does this mean I don't have to lead my family? Or bring up godly conversation in the home? Or teach my kids about God? Should I leave that up to someone else? I bet you already know my answer! Heck, no! It is my responsibility.

You might not be a pastor like me, but I bet if you are a young parent you can relate to being tired. I have many long, hard days at work and the last thing that I want to do when I get home is be Mr. Dad. Fortunately my kids are a bit older these days, but it wasn't too long ago that our evenings included changing diapers, feeding my kids food they don't like, hearing them fuss about it, throwing them into the bath, putting their pajamas on, reading bedtime stories and praying with one while the other one makes a mess, helping clean up the mess, praying with the second child, tucking him in, and finally being able to rest. You have moments of joy and excitement with children, but sometimes taking care of my kids is the last thing I want to do.

And yet, even in the midst of all of it, I find parenting satisfying. There is this sense that I'm doing what God has called me to do right now. Sometimes pouring into your family and being a presence at home is difficult, yet when we are present and following God in these roles, we are satisfied.

You've probably heard some statistics about how important family time is. Yet it seems families are spending less and less quality time together.

Time magazine posted this insight: "Studies show that the more often families eat together, the less likely kids are to smoke, drink, do drugs, get depressed, develop eating disorders and consider suicide, and the more likely they are to do well in school, delay having sex, eat their vegetables, learn big words and know which fork to use."[42] It may not sound like a big deal to have a family dinner together, but clearly it's important. And what's most important is spending time together doing things that glorify God.

In these moments, we can tell our kids about God and what He's done. He has sent His Son Jesus to die on the cross for our sins so we might have grace and be ushered into a life where we want to follow after Him! That's the most amazing gift we could ever ask for! He's done a lot of other things for us as well. Who better to share that with than our own family?

It doesn't matter what our job is. It doesn't matter how tired we are. We are called to be witnesses, and especially in our own family. **Before we go out and proclaim to the world who God is, let's first remember that we are living out our faith in our home.** How can you be a better witness of God's love today? Are there ways you can engage in godly conversation more often? Do you pray with your spouse? All of these questions are good to consider when talking about declaring what God has done in our homes.

BEFORE WE GO OUT AND PROCLAIM TO THE WORLD WHO GOD IS, LET'S FIRST REMEMBER THAT WE ARE LIVING OUT OUR FAITH IN OUR HOME.

In this story, Jesus meets a demon-possessed man and heals him. The natural response for the man who was healed was to proclaim what Jesus had done to everyone, including his family!

LUKE 8:27-33, 37B-39

27 As Jesus was getting out of the boat, he was met by a man from that town. The man had demons in him. He had gone naked for a long time and no longer lived in a house, but in the graveyard.

28 The man saw Jesus and screamed. He knelt down in front of him and shouted, "Jesus, Son of God in heaven, what do you want with me? I beg you not to torture me!" 29 He said this because Jesus had already told the evil spirit to go out of him.

The man had often been attacked by the demon. And even though he had been bound with chains and leg irons and kept under guard, he smashed whatever bound him. Then the demon would force him out into lonely places.
30 Jesus asked the man, "What is your name?"

He answered, "My name is Lots." He said this because there were 'lots' of demons in him. 31 They begged Jesus not to send them to the deep pit, where they would be punished.

32 A large herd of pigs was feeding there on the hillside. So the demons begged Jesus to let them go into the pigs, and Jesus let them go. 33 Then the demons left the man and went into the pigs. The whole herd rushed down the steep bank into the lake and drowned.

37 When Jesus got into the boat to start back, 38 the man who had been healed begged to go with him. But Jesus sent him off and said, 39 "Go back home and tell everyone how much God has done for you." The man then went all over town, telling everything that Jesus had done for him.

AT SOME POINT TODAY, GATHER YOUR FAMILY OR ROOMMATES OR FRIENDS AND SHARE WHAT GOD HAS DONE FOR YOU.

This might be over dinner. Pray with your family and have everyone in the family pray at least one sentence. Try doing this as a family for a week. If you don't know what to pray, you can start by thanking Him for all the things He has given to you and done for you.

34/40

DAY 35

How many times have you heard your mom say, "Don't ever take candy from a stranger?" Though she said it with good intentions, it sent us the message that we should be afraid of strangers. And now Jesus is telling me that rather than running and being fearful of strangers, I should welcome them instead?

Have you ever moved somewhere and nobody welcomed you? Or have you had the opposite happen: you've moved to a new place and someone went above and beyond to meet you and make you feel welcome?

I remember a couple of years ago a new family moved in down the street from us. I didn't think anything of it, but my amazing wife wanted to welcome them. She baked them some sort of organic pumpkin bread (which I actually didn't like - I thought she should just give them something like regular, sugary, non-organic brownies or cookies). But they received the bread and whether or not they actually liked it, they really appreciated that someone welcomed them!

It's not the quality of the bread but the gesture that counts! And, wouldn't you know it, a relationship blossomed from that pumpkin bread and now they are a regular part of our church family and good friends!

I'm convinced the best way to grow the church and build God's Kingdom is to continue meeting new people and getting involved in the community. If we become a Christian and surround ourselves with great Christian friends and only hang out with other Christians, it becomes harder and harder to expand outside of those Christian circles. But God never calls us to a life of comfort, safety, and ease. Instead, He calls us to a life that pushes us out of our comfort zone. For whatever reason, this is difficult, especially when it comes to forming new relationships and meeting new people.

What I've discovered, however, is that the more I push myself out of my comfort zone, the more God shows up. One of the nicknames of the Holy Spirit is the "Great Comforter." You don't need the Holy Spirit if you never leave the comfort zone. But when you go beyond the levels of your comfort, you experience parts of God you would otherwise miss.

One of my goals this past year was to get even more involved in the community and continue to foster new relationships. Over the past year I've grown really close to a group of guys I met while playing racquetball and volleyball, I've met a lot more of my neighbors, and I've taken part in many other activities outside of the church. This year I'm hoping to get more involved with my HOA and I'm looking for even more ways to meet new people. Have you made this a similar priority in your life? If not, why not? If you don't ever meet anybody new, how will the Kingdom of God grow through you?

It's not as hard as it sounds. What do you enjoy doing? You have interests and others have interests too. I love to play golf, so I schedule a monthly tee time for a group and it is a great chance to invite both those already in the church and those who have no connection with a church. As we play golf, we get to know one another. The Christians in the group don't beat the non-Christian over the head with our golf clubs telling him about how loving and gracious our God is - we just play golf. And as a follower of Jesus, I wait for the Spirit to prompt me for when I might say a particular word about God or our church.

But how do I know when the Spirit might prompt me? If you are in His Word on a daily basis like you have been in this Challenge, you will be in tune with God in such a way that you will know when the Spirit wants you to say something or do something that will make an impact in another person's life.

I want to encourage you today to get more involved, especially with people you may not know yet. You never know where God might lead your relationship. You shouldn't take candy from a stranger as a child, but it's okay to go ahead and meet one as an adult!

WHEN YOU GO BEYOND THE LEVELS OF YOUR COMFORT...
YOU EXPERIENCE PARTS OF GOD YOU WOULD OTHERWISE MISS.

In this story, Jesus chooses a tax collector (someone who would have been an outcast) to follow Him and then dines with the other tax collectors and sinners. In this story, we see that Jesus welcomed all people, even strangers, into relationship with Him.

MATTHEW 9:9-13

9 As Jesus went on from there, he saw a man named Matthew sitting at the tax collector's booth. "Follow me," he told him, and Matthew got up and followed him.

10 While Jesus was having dinner at Matthew's house, many tax collectors and sinners came and ate with him and his disciples. 11 When the Pharisees saw this, they asked his disciples, "Why does your teacher eat with tax collectors and sinners?"

12 On hearing this, Jesus said, "It is not the healthy who need a doctor, but the sick. 13 But go and learn what this means: 'I desire mercy, not sacrifice.'

SAY HELLO TO SOME NEIGHBORS YOU HAVEN'T MET YET.

Or start/join a group in your neighborhood or community doing something you enjoy. Get in a new social circle! Meet new people. If this is too much for you to do on your own, ask a friend to accompany you.

35/40

DAY 36

These are the very last recorded words Jesus spoke to His disciples before He ascended into heaven. Jesus was very intentional about what He did and said throughout His ministry, and this includes these final words. These words are powerful and extremely important.

I remember when ESPN started showing high school basketball games. The first one I ever saw was Lebron James and his St. Vincent-St. Mary high school team. Right away you knew you were watching someone special. After his high school career was over he jumped right to the NBA. He was drafted by the Cleveland Cavaliers, which just so happened to be my favorite basketball team. Right away, when he came into the league, Nike signed him to a massive contract. One of their most popular slogans for Lebron James fans was "We are all witnesses." We were seeing someone and something special.

That's what a witness is. If you are in the courtroom and you are called as a witness, it is your job to testify and give evidence of what you know, what you have seen, or what you've heard. That is called your testimony. When Jesus calls us as His witnesses, it ought to be a comforting thing. When you are a witness you simply tell what you know and what you've seen. Sometimes we overthink things when it comes to the Christian faith. We get very nervous to talk about Jesus Christ to someone else or to speak about Him in public. We think we need to know the exact words to say and have answers to every question that someone might ask before we start talking about who Jesus is.

Each of us is unique and God has done extraordinary things for each of us by saving us from our sins and giving us eternal life. Beyond that, God has done so much else for us and each of us has a story to tell. **What has God done for you?** What difference has God made in your life? I believe answering those questions is far more effective than some of our evangelism strategies. People connect with you when they hear how God has made an impact in your litfe.

And there's something else comforting about being a witness for Jesus Christ. This comforting news actually comes earlier in the Acts 1:8 verse:

"But you will receive power when the Holy Spirit comes on you; and you will be my witnesses…"

When we witness, and **when we speak about Jesus Christ, we do not go alone.** We go with His Holy Spirit and His power. Many times in the Gospels, Jesus says that when we speak on His behalf His Holy Spirit will speak through us. He will give us the words to say.[43] When you testify about who Jesus is and what He has done for you, God's Spirit is given the opportunity to work powerfully and mightily through you. **Don't underestimate what God can do through you and your story.**

In this story, God has called Moses to be the rescuer and leader of the Israelite people. Moses feels unqualified, and makes an excuse that he's never been eloquent. God reminds Moses that it is He who gave him his mouth in the first place and that He will help him speak and teach him what to say. Whenever God calls us to do something, He always goes with us! We are never alone!

EXODUS 4:10-12

10 Moses said to the Lord, "Pardon your servant, Lord. I have never been eloquent, neither in the past nor since you have spoken to your servant. I am slow of speech and tongue."

11 The Lord said to him, "Who gave human beings their mouths? Who makes them deaf or mute? Who gives them sight or makes them blind? Is it not I, the Lord? 12 Now go; I will help you speak and will teach you what to say."

WRITE DOWN YOUR TESTIMONY.

If you are struggling with what to write, answer these two questions: What has God done for you? What difference has God made in your life?

_____

_____

_____

_____

_____

_____

_____

_____

36/40

DAY 37

One of the most influential books I've ever read is *Dallas Willard's The Divine Conspiracy*. Much of the book is based on Jesus' fundamental message - the Kingdom of God - and it describes what life in the Kingdom looks like. Willard talks about how often Jesus brought up the Kingdom of God and how important it is to us today. Willard describes the Kingdom of God as, "The free availability of God's rule and righteousness to all of humanity through reliance upon Jesus himself, the person now loose in the world among us."[44]

I want to explain to you what the Kingdom of God means for us and how important it is in our lives today. Many churches and pastors teach the "Gospel of Forgiveness of Sins." This is the Gospel that Jesus came, lived a perfect life, died on a cross for your sins, and now offers grace to you through forgiveness of your sins. If you believe in Jesus as your Savior, then all your sins are forgiven and you can enter into eternal life with Him. That is amazing news!

But it's only a piece of the Gospel. It's not the entirety of the Good News.

Consider this situation: An upright citizen and member of the church comes to his pastor and says, "I'm going to divorce my wife because I've fallen in love with someone else." The pastor, of course, would say, "You can't do this." The man says, "Of course I can, you've said that Jesus will forgive my sins if I believe that He died on the cross." What would you say next? What could you say next?

If all you had was the "Gospel of Forgiveness of Sins," then there's really no good response. Jesus would forgive him. Or would he? That's where the Kingdom of God comes in. The Kingdom of God teaches us that Christ came to offer forgiveness of sins and eternal life for all who believe, but it also teaches us that it's not just about forgiveness. The Kingdom of God is also reaping the benefits and rewards now because our eternal life has already started! And we get to participate with God in bringing the Kingdom of God to this world right now.

Here's how it works: I've made a mess of my life. God forgives me. I'm so compelled by Christ's kindness and grace that I can't help but want to serve Him with my life.

If we are really pursuing Jesus and believe in the reality of the Kingdom of God in us then we would never want to divorce our wife, because it's not right. We would never even pursue loving another woman if we were married because Christ or His disciples would never have done that!

There's the "Gospel of the Forgiveness of Sins" which is what makes us right before God and allows us to enter into eternal life with Him in heaven. And that's good news for the future. But there's also the "Gospel of the Kingdom of God" which gives us hope for today and compels us to become like Jesus today. We can look more and more like Jesus as we follow after Him and as we're led by the power of the Holy Spirit. Both Gospels are important, and to me, they are one and the same. I don't believe you can have one without the other.

Jesus began His ministry in Matthew 4 with these words: "Repent, for the kingdom of heaven is at hand." Jesus is announcing to us the availability of the Kingdom of God and inviting us all to be a part of that. He is saying, "Come one, come all. This invitation is open to all." He wants us all to be saved and live with Him in heaven forever. But even more importantly, He wants us to have good news today that God lives and reigns in you and **you can make a difference and bring His Kingdom right here and right now.**

YOU CAN MAKE A DIFFERENCE AND BRING HIS KINGDOM RIGHT HERE AND RIGHT NOW.

#REDLETTERCHALLENGE

Throughout the book of Acts, Paul is hoping to share the Gospel in Rome. Finally, after many unforeseen and unfortunate events he has the ability to preach in Rome under guard. As you can see from this short piece of Scripture, some people believed and others didn't. It's not up to you to determine what your words and your testimony produce, it's up to you to simply share your story. **Obedience is your responsibility. Outcome is God's responsibility.**

ACTS 28:23-31

23 They arranged to meet Paul on a certain day, and came in even larger numbers to the place where he was staying. He witnessed to them from morning till evening, explaining about the kingdom of God, and from the Law of Moses and from the Prophets he tried to persuade them about Jesus. 24 Some were convinced by what he said, but others would not believe. 25 They disagreed among themselves and began to leave after Paul had made this final statement: "The Holy Spirit spoke the truth to your ancestors when he said through Isaiah the prophet:

26 "'Go to this people and say, "You will be ever hearing but never understanding; you will be ever seeing but never perceiving." 27 For this people's heart has become calloused; they hardly hear with their ears, and they have closed their eyes. Otherwise they might see with their eyes, hear with their ears, understand with their hearts and turn, and I would heal them.'

28 "Therefore I want you to know that God's salvation has been sent to the Gentiles, and they will listen!" 30 For two whole years Paul stayed there in his own rented house and welcomed all who came to see him. 31 He proclaimed the kingdom of God and taught about the Lord Jesus Christ— with all boldness and without hindrance

RECORD A VIDEO OF THE TESTIMONY YOU WROTE YESTERDAY.

Share it on all your social media platforms. Please share it on our Facebook page as well: www.fb.me/redletterchallenge.

_____

_____

_____

_____

_____

_____

_____

37/40

DAY 38

GO INTO ALL THE WORLD AND
PREACH THE GOSPEL TO EVERY
CREATURE
MARK 16:15

This is a pretty intimidating quote. For many of us, the Red Letter Challenge
has gotten harder as it has gone on and now it's really ramping up! For some
people, this is where they will really need God's presence to go with them,
because they are afraid of telling someone about Jesus. They think, "I'll do
all the other things, I'll forgive, I'll serve, I'll be generous, but don't make me
open my mouth!"

St. Francis of Assisi once said, "Preach the Gospel, and if necessary, use
words." People love this quote. And I think it's great because it emphasizes
that our actions are very important when it comes to living out our faith.
But I think far too many people look at this quote and use it as an excuse to
never speak.

There is a time to show people who Jesus is through our actions, but there
is absolutely a time to speak as well. It's not an either/or, it's a both/and.
I need to both show people who God is through my actions and I need to
speak the Gospel.

We've lost our boldness when it comes to speaking about God. Many of us
would rather do anything else. But why is that? If God has truly died on the
cross for you and paid the price that you deserved to pay, if He has literally
rescued you from hell, wouldn't you want to share that good news with others?

My denomination came up with a long study of why church attendance, baptisms, and membership in our denomination is on a decline. The number one answer they came up with is that we are having fewer children. So even though the population is increasing, we've blamed our denominational decline on the birthrate?! The solution is to have more children? I found this ridiculous. We would rather raise a child from birth than actually go out there and tell somebody about Jesus!

I struggle with this because many times throughout Scripture God commands His people to proclaim who He is. Not only that, but He sends us with His Holy Spirit so we can have confidence. We don't have to go out with fear and timidity, but instead we operate from a position of power and strength.

I know it's not easy to speak in public or tell someone about Jesus. It's hard to talk in front of others. As a child, I really struggled with speaking in public. I always got so nervous. Because my last name was at the end of the alphabet, I was usually last and so I had even more time to worry. I remember silently rooting for other people to do miserable in their speeches just so mine wouldn't be as bad as everyone else's. I was terrified.

But **God can turn your fear into confidence.**

After enough speeches and sermons, I began to get confidence in this area. Now I love to speak in public. I love to preach. I love to tell people about Jesus. It's what I live for. In fact, a couple of years ago, I decided I was going to try to break a Guinness World Record for the longest speech of all time. I wanted to preach all the way through the Bible and help people understand God's Word better and, at the same time, use the event as a fundraiser for a new non-profit in our area to build a recovery home for men. 53 hours and 18 minutes later I was a Guinness World Record holder and am literally the longest-winded preacher of all time!

There were many times I didn't know what to say, but God came through in a mighty way. There were Bible verses I didn't know I had memorized that God gave me at three in the morning. That particular weekend was living proof for me that I just have to be obedient and show up and God will take care of the rest. He will speak when I don't know what to say.

When I do force myself to be uncomfortable, I experience God in ways I otherwise would have missed. He has always shown up. He never leaves you or forsakes you. There are far too many people out there who don't know Jesus Christ as their Lord and Savior. Increasing our birthrate is fine, but there are many people who are already here, already dying and going to hell. It is our job to both show and tell them who Jesus Christ is. Let's not wait. The stakes are too high.

GOD CAN TURN YOUR FEAR INTO CONFIDENCE.

God gave the prophet Ezekiel a vision and led him to a valley of dry bones. In this vision, he is surrounded by dry, dead, decomposing bodies. Talk about a tough crowd! This vision shows us that the Word of the Lord is effective. He can make dead bones live again and He can make spiritually dead people live again.

EZEKIEL 37:1-10

The hand of the Lord was on me, and he brought me out by the Spirit of the Lord and set me in the middle of a valley; it was full of bones. 2 He led me back and forth among them, and I saw a great many bones on the floor of the valley, bones that were very dry. 3 He asked me, "Son of man, can these bones live?"

I said, "Sovereign Lord, you alone know."

4 Then he said to me, "Prophesy to these bones and say to them, 'Dry bones, hear the word of the Lord! 5 This is what the Sovereign Lord says to these bones: I will make breath enter you, and you will come to life. 6 I will attach tendons to you and make flesh come upon you and cover you with skin; I will put breath in you, and you will come to life. Then you will know that I am the Lord.'"

7 So I prophesied as I was commanded. And as I was prophesying, there was a noise, a rattling sound, and the bones came together, bone to bone. 8 I looked, and tendons and flesh appeared on them and skin covered them, but there was no breath in them.

9 Then he said to me, "Prophesy to the breath; prophesy, son of man, and say to it, 'This is what the Sovereign Lord says: Come, breath, from the four winds and breathe into these slain, that they may live.'" 10 So I prophesied as he commanded me, and breath entered them; they came to life and stood up on their feet—a vast army.

WRITE DOWN FIVE PEOPLE IN YOUR LIFE WHO DO NOT HAVE A RELATIONSHIP WITH JESUS CHRIST.

Talk to one of those five today about your testimony. Make a plan over the next month to speak with the other four. This should go without saying, but make sure when you talk with them that you are also there to listen to them about anything they may be going through.

38/40

DAY 39

As you've been going through the 40-day Challenge, I hope you've had some victories. But if you are like me, you've struggled at times. There are times in my relationship with God when I wonder if I have what it takes to truly follow after Him the way He wants me to.

As we wrap up this Challenge, remember that God loves you for who you are. God chose you to be His son or His daughter before the foundations of the world even existed and before you ever did a thing. You don't have to earn your way into a relationship with God. **And He has not chosen you because of your effort or because you've done anything important, but simply because He loves you.**

When you follow Jesus, there will be days that you struggle. There will be days that won't go as planned. The Christian walk is not easy by any means. But even when you fail, it does not disqualify you from being a follower of Jesus.

With only a couple of days left, I want to remind you that God is the one who gives you your identity. Who you think you are will determine what decisions you make and how you live your life. Your identity determines your biography. And your identity was given to you by God and it was confirmed when your sins were nailed to the cross. Why would we look to anyone or anything other than God for our identity?

A decade ago one of my favorite shows was "American Idol." What I loved most about it was seeing some of the musicians realize their dreams. It broke my heart to see people that thought they were good actually be told by Simon Cowell that they were in fact one of the worst singers in the world!

After the success of "American Idol", reality singing shows became very popular. And they were all very similar: A bunch of people trying to hit it big and usually singing in front of an audience that included at least three judges, one of whom had to be British.

Then a new show came out called "The Voice." It was a signing contest with an exciting twist. In the very first round, called the "Blind Audition Round" the singers would perform in front of four celebrity judges, but the twist was, the judges couldn't see them. Their backs were turned to the singers.

As they poured out everything they had on the stage, the judges would listen and if they liked the singer, they would then hit a button forcing their chair to turn around. Then a light would shine across the bottom of the chair displaying these words: "I want you." That meant the judge liked hearing them so much that they picked them, sight unseen, to be on his or her team. It's quite an honor to be chosen by one of the top musical talents in the world.[46]

It's awesome to see someone realize their dream. It's great to see someone hand-picked. Sometimes all four chairs turned around with all of the judges wanting the singer on their team. What made the show fun is to see these celebrity judges fight over who gets to be the singer's coach. But what's tough is when the singer didn't get anyone to turn their chair around. Nobody wanted them. Nobody has chosen them. Rejected.

Similarly, I think a lot of us go through our lives like these contestants do. We are auditioning for everyone around us. We are trying to win the approval of whoever the judges are that we've appointed to sit in chairs we've furnished in our minds. We keep thinking of ways to get the people in our lives to like us more. To approve of our lives. Ways to get more Facebook likes. More Instagram followers.

We try really hard and we run really fast to do all that we can to gain approval in this world. And the craziest part about all of this is that the God who made us has already chosen us and already loves us, not based on how well we sing, or based on anything we can do in this world. In fact, before we even audition, God has not just turned his chair around, but He's already come down off his seat from the throne room of heaven to declare "I want you."

"God has issued an announcement from His throne in heaven, and He wants you to know, The audition has been canceled. He has not chosen you blindly but intentionally, even while knowing you inwardly and intimately. And let me tell you why this is some of the best news in the history of the universe: If this God has chosen you while totally knowing even the worst parts of you, then you no longer have to live up to anyone or "anything!"[47]

Inside all of us, I believe God has placed a deep longing for something more, for significance. That "something more" is truly following after Him.

No matter how you've done in this Challenge, God still loves you. And He's still chosen you. Don't get defeated and frustrated. Get right back up and keep moving! You've got a story to tell.

HE CHOSE YOU NOT BECAUSE YOU'VE DONE ANYTHING IMPORTANT, BUT SIMPLY BECAUSE HE LOVES YOU.

In this section, God tells Jeremiah that He handpicked him for His task. God made His choice not after Jeremiah proved his potential as a preacher or after Jeremiah demonstrated significant levels of consistency. Rather, God chose Jeremiah before he was even born. Before Jeremiah could do anything to merit God's acceptance, He hit the big button!

JEREMIAH 1:4-10

4 The word of the Lord came to me, saying,

5 "Before I formed you in the womb I knew you,
before you were born I set you apart;
I appointed you as a prophet to the nations."

6 "Alas, Sovereign Lord," I said, "I do not know how to speak; I am too young."

7 But the Lord said to me, "Do not say, 'I am too young.' You must go to everyone I send you to and say whatever I command you. 8 Do not be afraid of them, for I am with you and will rescue you," declares the Lord.

9 Then the Lord reached out his hand and touched my mouth and said to me, "I have put my words in your mouth. 10 See, today I appoint you over nations and kingdoms to uproot and tear down, to destroy and overthrow, to build and to plant."

JUST AS GOD CHOSE YOU BEFORE YOU EVER DID ANYTHING TO PLEASE HIM,

I want you to choose someone today who hasn't done anything to earn your favor and find a way to bless that person.

_____

_____

_____

_____

_____

_____

_____

39/40

DAY 40

Following Jesus is the greatest opportunity we will ever have!

The disciples understood this. It's why they immediately followed Jesus.
I don't think we understand how special it is to be a disciple of Jesus. The way I
thought of a disciple changed when I studied Ray Vanderlaan's work entitled
"Dust of the Rabbi." Much of this devotion comes from his teachings.

To understand what a disciple is one must go back to the time Jesus was
born. Jesus was born in Israel, and the people who were most highly
regarded and respected in Israel were those who taught the Torah, the first
five books of the Old Testament. A teacher of the Torah was known as a
rabbi. This was a highly respected position. In the New Testament, Jesus
was referred to as a rabbi 14 times and as a teacher 40 times.

Vanderlaan says that, *"For a young boy growing up in Israel, to be a rabbi
was the greatest thing that could happen to you"*[48] The second- greatest
thing would be to become a follower of a rabbi, especially Rabbi Jesus.
There was something special about Rabbi Jesus. Not only did He teach
the Torah with full understanding, He also spoke with authority over the
wind and the waves. He began to heal many people and do other miracles.
Imagine how exciting it must have been to become one of His disciples.

However, it usually took a great deal of work to become a disciple of a rabbi. One rabbi from Jesus' day wrote this: *"Under the age of six we do not receive a child. But from six upwards, we accept him and stuff him with Torah like an ox"*[49] At age six a little boy could go to *Bet Sefer*, the house of the book. From age six to age ten, a little boy would literally sit at the feet of a teacher and memorize Torah. By the time he was 10 years old, the young Jewish boy would have all of Genesis, Exodus, Leviticus, Numbers, and Deuteronomy memorized.

At this point, many boys would return home to learn a trade. Some students, however, had a special gift, and they'd be accepted to move on to the next level: *Bet Talmud*, the house of learning. They would keep memorizing, day after day, year after year. And by the age of 14, it wasn't uncommon for these students to have the entire Hebrew Scripture memorized - Genesis through Malachi, more than a thousand pages in my Bible! And their rabbi would ask them questions of understanding. For these disciples it wasn't just knowing what was in the text; they had to be able to interpret it as well. It had to be part of their life.

At the age of 14 or 15, the best of the best from *Bet Talmud* would find a rabbi they admired and ask to be one of his students. The rabbi would then give them a test. If they passed it, he would accept them and they would begin the *Bet Midrash*, the house of study.

At this point the students would spend every waking minute with their rabbi to learn from him. This is what it took to become a disciple back then! Only the best of the best made it.

But the disciples Jesus chose weren't the best of the best. He didn't wait for people to ask to follow Him. Instead, He went to a tax collector named Matthew. He went to guys who didn't make it through rabbi school, unschooled and ordinary men like Peter, Andrew, James, and John. These people didn't deserve to follow after the greatest rabbi ever! These guys were used to failing. Can you imagine how excited they were to get the call from Jesus? This was the greatest opportunity of their lives!

A rabbi of that day would bless a student with these words: **"May you be covered by the dust of your rabbi."** In other words, may you follow your rabbi so closely that when his feet kick up dust, it covers you.

Do you want to go and make disciples? Live in the dust of Jesus. It'll happen.

FOLLOWING JESUS IS THE GREATEST OPPORTUNITY WE WILL EVER HAVE!

#REDLETTERCHALLENGE

Here we have the story of Jesus calling one of His disciples. What an honor and privilege to be chosen by Rabbi Jesus!

LUKE 5:27-32

27 After this, Jesus went out and saw a tax collector by the name of Levi sitting at his tax booth. "Follow me," Jesus said to him, 28 and Levi got up, left everything and followed him.

29 Then Levi held a great banquet for Jesus at his house, and a large crowd of tax collectors and others were eating with them. 30 But the Pharisees and the teachers of the law who belonged to their sect complained to his disciples, "Why do you eat and drink with tax collectors and sinners?"

31 Jesus answered them, "It is not the healthy who need a doctor, but the sick. 32 I have not come to call the righteous, but sinners to repentance."

IT IS IMPERATIVE THAT YOU BECOME A DISCIPLE, OR FOLLOWER, OF JESUS.

If you aren't already, can you identify one or two people who are mature disciples of Jesus and ask them to mentor you? If you are already a mature follower of Jesus Christ, seek out one or two people you could mentor.

_____

_____

_____

_____

_____

_____

40/40

DAY 41 AND ON

Now that you have completed the Challenge, how did it go? If you are like me, you were probably stronger in some areas than others. I hope over the past 40 days you have learned more about God and what He asks of His followers. You can repeat the Challenge as often as you'd like and compare how it went each time. The Challenge is for a lifetime, because **when we follow Jesus and His words, we find the life we were made for.**

I encourage you to continue pursuing the five main principles of this Challenge: Being, Forgiving, Serving, Giving, and Going. Following Jesus well is a combination of these five principles. I also encourage you to get connected with a local church and a small group of like-minded Jesus-followers. It is not always easy to follow Jesus, and you will need the support and encouragement from others to keep going. Not only that, but others will need your support and encouragement as well!
Let me leave you with this blessing:

→

MAY YOU PURSUE JESUS WITH ALL YOUR HEART, MAY GOD USE YOU TO DO MIGHTY THINGS FOR HIS KINGDOM, AND AFTER ALL IS SAID AND DONE IN THIS WORLD, MAY YOU HEAR GOD SAY TO YOU, "WELL DONE, MY GOOD AND FAITHFUL SERVANT."

SELF-REFLECTION

Following Jesus is the greatest opportunity we will ever have, and it's also something we constantly want to strive to get better at. So how'd you do? Give yourself an honest assessment for each of the five main principles by rating yourself on a scale of 1-10, 1 being the worst, 10 being the best.

Being

1   2   3   4   5   6   7   8   9   10

Forgiving

1   2   3   4   5   6   7   8   9   10

Serving

1   2   3   4   5   6   7   8   9   10

Giving

1   2   3   4   5   6   7   8   9   10

Going

1   2   3   4   5   6   7   8   9   10

FINAL TAKEAWAYS

What is your biggest strength and your biggest weakness when it comes to following the Red Letters of Jesus?

_____

_____

_____

_____

_____

_____

_____

_____

_____

_____

ABOUT THE AUTHOR

TWITTER: @ZACHZEHNDER

Zach completed his undergraduate work at Concordia University Wisconsin. It was there that he met his wife Allison, and they were married in July 2004. From there, Zach earned his Masters of Divinity from Concordia Seminary, St. Louis, MO in May 2010. Zach and Allison have two boys: Nathan and Brady. In May 2010, Zach accepted a call to plant a church in Mount Dora, FL called theCross. In just a few short years, the church has grown from just his family to several hundreds and is currently the fastest-growing church in the Lutheran Church—Missouri Synod.

Zach has made worldwide news for his creative ways of doing ministry. In April 2014, Zach made a sarcastic remark in one of his sermons that he would pay for people to get a tattoo of their church's logo as a way to help advertise. While he was just joking about this, it turned out to be a real thing as 21 people got tattooed with the logo and the story went viral!

But that sermon is not the most famous one Zach has preached. In November 2014, Zach broke the Guinness World Record for the Longest Speech Marathon by an individual. Zach preached for 53 hours and 18 minutes and weaved his way from Genesis to Revelation all without having a Bible in front of him (per Guinness rules). The event raised over $100,000 for a non-profit to buy a house for a men's recovery program. The program now has more than 20 men going through at once.

His hobbies include travel, reading, volleyball, golf, basketball, ping-pong, and entrepreneurial ventures. Zach started a business in his dorm room selling golf headcovers and sold over 150,000 golf headcovers.

ACKNOW LEDGE MENTS

I'm extremely grateful for Allison, my wife! She has been so supportive of our ministry from the time I met her and has also challenged me in my faith in so many different ways. This book would not have happened without her! I'm so grateful to my kids Nathan and Brady for providing so many stories and so much material. God has big plans for both of you and I can't wait to see all that you will do!

I'm thankful for my parents, Mark and Sharon, who demonstrated first-hand what it looks like to follow Jesus. My siblings, Eric and Charista, have been extremely supportive of me. Your support means the world to me. My new family, the Buck family, is filled with love, support, and encouragement. Thank you!

I'm blessed to know the Thrasher family. You guys have gotten behind this project in a way that I will never forget. Thank you for your undying support and love!

I'm grateful and excited for the church I serve. At theCross, we truly have become a family of faith-filled, big-thinking followers of Jesus Christ. Thank you for being serious about reaching out to the community and practicing the Red Letters on a daily basis. I love being your pastor.

I'm grateful for the team of people at theCross that I work with in Florida. It's a ton of fun seeing people's lives change for Jesus! Special thanks to Jacob Baumann, Mark Crossman, Chris Burns, Kevin Lang, and the crew for all your over and above time and support with this project!

I'm grateful for the team at Plain Joe Studios. Peter McGowan, Kim Jetton, Kai Husen, Blake Ryan: Thank you for believing in this project and helping my dream become a reality.

All glory goes to Jesus Christ, who is crazy enough to give me the opportunity to follow after Him. It is not a burden to follow after Him, but the single greatest opportunity of my lifetime!

APPENDIX

COMMUNITY RALLY IDEAS

Following Jesus was never meant to be done alone. During the Red Letter Challenge, we encourage you to not only do the Challenge together, but also organize community rallies around particular words of Jesus. Rallies are opportunities for groups to come together and make great impact in the community. Here are several examples of how your church could pair certain words of Jesus with a community rally.

Abide in my Word: Host a special Bible study at the church.

Pray earnestly: Host a prayer walk. Gather everyone together and give them ideas and things to pray for.

Worship the Lord Your God: Organize a special worship service to equip and empower people to stay strong in the Challenge.

Let us eat and celebrate: Plan a massive party and invite the community to be part of it.

When you give a dinner, invite the poor, crippled, lame, etc.: Put on a fish fry in the community and invite those who are less fortunate.

Love your neighbor as yourself: Organize a team to go through a neighborhood and clean up people's yards and houses.

Let the little children come to me: Organize an event at a children's hospital or camp to encourage and entertain the children.

I was sick and you took care of me: Organize an event at a local hospital to encourage those who are sick.

Let your light shine before others: Organize a work day with an organization like Habitat for Humanity.

For I was hungry and you gave me food: Organize a food drive for your church or a volunteer work day at a local food pantry.

I was naked and you gave me clothing: Organize a clothing drive at the church and give away the clothes to a local shelter.

Go and proclaim the Kingdom of God: Organize an event to go through the city or neighborhoods and pass out information on who Jesus is and how people can connect to your local church. As you are going, pray for the people you come in contact with.

BIBLIO
GRAPHY

1 Gallo, D.J. "Allen Iverson's Practice Rant: 10 Years Later." espn.com. n.p. 7 May 2012. Web. 31 August 2013.

2 Dibs to Francis Chan and one of his past sermons for giving me this sermon illustration!

3 Illustration taken from Freeway: A Not so Perfect Guide to Freedom.

4 Manning, Brennan. The Ragamuffin Gospel. Sisters, Or.: Multnomah, 2000. 2.

5 Ibid, 14.

6 2 Kings 4:13

7 Furtick, Steven. Upon Further Review. player.subsplash.com/1a20599. 22 September 2012. Web. 25 January 2017.

8 Packer, Michael. "Jesus Talked the Most About Money." patch.com. n.p. 24 July 2011. Web. January 2017.

9 Stanley, Andy. "Your Move with Andy Stanley: Be Rich: Episode 2, Side Effects." yourmove.is. n.p. 3 November 2013. Web. 25 January 2017.

10 Haugen, Gary. Just Courage: God's Great Expedition for the Restless Christian. Downers Grove, IL: InterVarsity Press, 2008. Pgs. 7-16.

11 Miller, Donald. A Million Miles in a Thousand Years. Nashville, TN: Thomas Nelson, 2009. Author's Note.

12 Weber, Jeremy. " 80% of Churchgoers Don't Read Bible Daily, LifeWay Survey Suggests." christianitytoday.com. n.p. 7 September 2012. Web. 14 June 2013

13 Schulz, Andrea. "Pray Big." willdavisjr.com. n.p. n.d. Web. 5 June 2013.

14 Foster, Richard J. Prayer: Finding the Heart's True Home. San Francisco: HarperCollins, 1992. Pg. 8.

15 Definition of worship. thefreedictionary.com. n.p. n.d. Web. 11 May 2012.

16 Best, Harold M. Music through the Eyes of Faith. San Francisco: HarperCollins, 1993. Pg. 147.

17 Worship quotes. cuttingitstraight.co.uk. n.p. n.d. Web. 4 January 2012.

18 Ireland, Michael. New Study Finds even Pastors are 'Too Busy for God'. christianity.org. n.p. 7 August 2007. Web. 1 May 2012.

19 Willard, Dallas. The Great Omission. [San Francisco]: HarperCollins, 2006. Pg. 38.

20 Keller, Timothy J. The Reason for God: Belief in an Age of Skepticism. New York: Dutton, 2008. 36.

21 Manning, Brennan. The Ragamuffin Gospel. Sisters, Or.: Multnomah, 2000. 149.

22 Exodus 31:13, ESV

23 Stevenson, John. Sabbath Controversies. angelfire.com/nt/theology. n.p. n.d. Web. 15 July 2013.

24 Paul Copan. True for You, But not for Me, (Minneapolis, MN: Bethany House Publishers, 1998) p.32-33. cites D.A. Carson, The Sermon on the Mount (Grand Rapids, Mich: Baker, 1978), page 97.

25 Matthew 7:3

26 Definition of mercy. Oxforddictionaries.com. n.p. n.d. Web.7 February 2012.

27 Zahnd, Brian. Unconditional? The Call of Jesus to Radical Forgiveness. Lake Mary, FL: Charisma House, 2010. Pg.18.

28 Wiesenthal, Simon. The Sunflower (New York: Schocken, 1997). Pgs. 14-15.

29 Matthew 18:3

30 "How do you Re-salt the Salt." sermons.logos.com. n.p. 1 October 2006. Web. 5 June 2012.

31 Levitt, Stephen D., and Stephen J. Dubner. Super Freakonomics. N.p.: HarperCollins Canada, Limited, 2009. Pgs. 121-122.

32 Sagal, Peter. Wait, Wait, the Moth and Theatre and Mother Theresa. Weplaydifferent.wordpress.com. n.p. 20 Jan 2012. Web. 5 May 2012.

33 Stanley, Andy. Deep & Wide: Creating Churches Unchurched People Love to Attend. Grand Rapids, MI: Zondervan, 2012. Pg. 125.

34 Aubrey, Allison. "The Average American Ate (Literally) A Ton This Year." npr.org. n.p. 31 December 2011. Web. 4 April 2013.

35 Gillam, Carey, & Grebler, Dan, ed. "Food Waste: Americans Throw Away Nearly Half Their Food, $165 Billion Annually, Study Says." huffingtonpost.com. n.p. 21 August 2012. Web. 17 May 2013.

36 Matthew 25:35-40

37 "A Rich Man Goes to Heaven." whosoever.org. n.p. n.d. Web. 15 April 2012.

38 Matthew 6:21

39 Bell, Rob and Don Golden. Jesus Wants to Save Christians. Grand Rapids, MI: Zondervan, 2012 Multiple pages.

40 Fernandez, Alvaro. 'Tis better to give than receive': oxytocin and dopamine. Sharpbrains.com. n.p. 21 Mar 2007. Web. 14 Mar 2009.

41 Dibs to Ben Hoyer on this quote. Ben is a great pastor and friend and many of his thoughts are echoed in my own words in this book.

42 Cabrera, Derek. "A family that eats together." thinknation.org. n.p. 2 April 2013. Web. 2 July 2013.

43 Matthew 10:20, Luke 12:12, John 14:26

44 Willard, Dallas. The Divine Conspiracy: Rediscovering Our Hidden Life in God. San Francisco: HarperSanFrancisco, 1998. Pg. 116.

45 Willard, Dallas & Giles, Keith. "The Gospel of the Kingdom." dwillard.org. n.p. 5 May 2010. Web. 5 Jun 2012.

46 Furtick, S. (2014). Crash the Chatterbox: Hearing God's Voice Above All Others [Kindle for iPhone version]. Retrieved from Amazon.com.

47 Ibid.

48 You can find Ray Vander Laan's teaching sat the website followtherabbi.com. This website is a great resource to understand how things were in the times in which Jesus lived and walked. It brings a lot of life to some of the stories and parables that Jesus teaches when you understand the context of where it came from.

49 Ibid.